Papers on Presidential Disability and the Twenty-Fifth Amendment

by Six Medical, Legal and Political Authorities

Edited by
KENNETH W. THOMPSON

D1158656

PAPERS ON PRESIDENTIAL DISABILITY and the TWENTY-FIFTH AMENDMENT

by Six Medical, Legal and Political Authorities

Edited by
Kenneth W. Thompson

Funded by the W. Alton Jones Foundation

University Press of America

Lanham • New York • London

The Miller Center

University of Virginia

Copyright © 1988 by
University Press of America,® Inc.

4720 Boston Way
Lanham, MD 20706

3 Henrietta Street
London WC2E 8LU England

Printed in the United States of America

British Cataloging in Publication Information Available

ISBN 0–8191–6921–8 (pbk. : alk. paper)
ISBN 0–8191–6920–X (alk. paper)

Co-published by arrangement with
The White Burkett Miller Center of Public Affairs,
University of Virginia

All University Press of America books are produced on acid-free
paper which exceeds the minimum standards set by the National
Historical Publications and Records Commission.

Dedicated

to

Kenneth R. Crispell, M.D.

whose work informed and inspired

the creation

of

the Miller Center Commission

on

Presidential Disability

and

the Twenty-fifth Amendment

Table of Contents

Annex A

PREFACE

The Miller Center of Public Affairs of the University of Virginia has a twofold mandate: to seek understanding of the American presidency through study and research and to foster the improvement of the presidency. Specifically, in research the Center has sought to further the understanding of the presidency through the valued contributions of scholars in residence at the Center. In public affairs, the main instrumentality for advancing ideas on the improvement of the presidency has been a series of four national commissions whose membership has comprised public figures and professional staff from the University of Virginia.

The Miller Center Commission on Presidential Disability and the Twenty-fifth Amendment is the fourth of the national commissions organized by the Center. Co-chairmen of the commission are the two principal authors of the Twenty-fifth Amendment: the Honorable Herbert Brownell, who served as attorney general in the Eisenhower administration, and former Senator Birch Bayh of Indiana. Its recommendations were drafted by former *Washington Post* Washington correspondent Chalmers M. Roberts. The Commission's vice-chairman is the Honorable Mortimer Caplin, director of the Internal Revenue Service in the Kennedy administration.

As with the preceding three commissions of the Center, the present commission's studies were staffed and administered by University of Virginia faculty. Professionals at the University who are qualified in the subject matter of the commission prepared papers which were made available to the commission. The authors of the papers also presented them to an audience of the wider university community and Miller Center family in Forums and Rotunda Lectures.

In keeping with the Center's public responsibility, the present volume was organized to facilitate the dissemination

PREFACE

of these papers to an even wider audience. In the past, we have published the working papers associated with the previous three commissions. With the present subject which links medicine, law, ethics and politics, the responsibility of making specific studies available seems even more important. Their publication is possible thanks to the generous funding of the W. Alton Jones Foundation and its president, R. Jeffrey Kelleher and the Center's co-publishing arrangement with the University Press of America and its outstanding leader, James E. Lyons. Finally, I should observe that the prime mover in introducing the Center to this subject and guiding us to undertake the study is Dr. Kenneth Crispell, former dean and vice president for Health Affairs of the University of Virginia Medical School. We respectfully dedicate this volume to him.

INTRODUCTION

A volume of papers on the subject of Presidential Disability and the Twenty-fifth Amendment is a vital part of the Miller Center's inquiry and its recommendations. Few subjects lend themselves as unmistakably to interdisciplinary review and discussion. The lines of study intersect and overlap drawing upon medical, legal and political approaches. Subjects such as the confidentiality relationship between the president and the presidential physician pose moral dilemmas that are not easily resolved. Each aspect of the problem to be studied calls for a high level of professional competence. Questions of disabling illnesses are not appropriate for amateur diagnosis or prognosis. Historians argue that the ability to govern is more than a medical judgment. Politics, law and medicine come together in any analysis of presidential disability. Constitutional questions arise in the interpretation and implementation of the Twenty-fifth Amendment.

For these reasons, the Miller Center turned to a group of outstanding medical, legal and political authorities to broaden and deepen understanding on presidential disability. With one exception, all are respected faculty at the University of Virginia. The one exception is former Indiana Senator Birch Bayh, who is recognized to have been a principal draftsmen and author of the Amendment. The other contributors are chair holders and distinguished professors in leading departments and schools at the University.

At the beginning of its study of the Twenty-fifth Amendment, the Center invited Senator Bayh to come to Charlottesville to discuss its history and meaning. He graciously consented to meet with the staff and spend a day explaining its origin and main provisions. Senator Bayh's grasp of the legislative history of the Amendment is unrivaled. He prepared the participants for their task as no one else could have done. Most importantly, he directed attention to political realities with which he and his fellow draftsman, the Honorable Herbert Brownell, had to be concerned. It is no exaggeration to say that Birch Bayh put his stamp on the work of the Miller Center Commission from the start through the extended presentation and colloquium he conducted at the Miller Center. As a Washington insider—Senator Bayh is a member of a leading Washington law firm—he guided the thinking of staff along lines that a purely academic inquiry in law or medicine might not have followed.

Dr. Kenneth Crispell followed Senator Bayh and his authorship of the Miller Center study merits recognition. Not only is Dr. Crispell highly respected in the medical community—he was dean and the vice president for Health Affairs at the University of Virginia Medical School—but he has studied the health of presidents throughout his medical career as his forthcoming book on hidden illnesses of presidents attests. Dr. Crispell introduced the director and staff of the Center to the subject. He helped overcome the skepticism of historians and political scientists to an inquiry into the subject. The fact is that the Miller Center would probably not have turned its attention to presidential disability if it had not been for the gentle persuasion and continuing educational efforts of Dr. Crispell. We respectfully dedicate this volume to him and his good natured and tireless indoctrination of his social science and humanities friends.

Paul B. Stephan III is a brilliant young legal scholar who is a professor at the University of Virginia Law School. Second only to Senator Bayh, Professor Stephan quietly and without fanfare mastered the last detail of the legislative history of the Twenty-fifth Amendment. He served as counsel to the Miller Center Commission preparing numerous drafts on important issues before the Commission (these drafts are now a part of the permanent archives of the Center). Stephan along with Professor Daniel Meador of the Law faculty constituted the legal expertise of the staff component of the project. His presentation explores some of the fundamental issues of the Amendment which preoccupied the Commission throughout its study.

INTRODUCTION

Dr. C. Knight Aldrich is both a leading American psychiatrist and a literary figure of repute. His paper entitled "Memory, Information and Denial in Public Life" is one of the most outstanding pieces of writing published by the Center. It is the type of analysis any professor in any field would be proud to see appear under his name. Aldrich's paper might well prompt a reader to say: "I wish I had written that." It provides a kind of textbook or scholarly treatise example of how to make clear and understandable to the public a complex and difficult subject. From the founding of the Center, Dr. Aldrich and his wife have been among its most loyal and informed supporters. Aldrich also was among those who urged the Center to undertake this study.

Not only Dr. Aldrich but also Dr. Norman J. Knorr, until recently dean of the University of Virginia Medical School, and his co-author, Dr. Daniel Harrington have contributed a significant and authoritative paper on mental and emotional illness. If the present volume contained only the papers by Drs. Aldrich, Knorr and Harrington, it would represent a landmark contribution to knowledge. The Commission's most difficult problem was to understand not physical but mental and emotional disability. Most presidential physicians are far more qualified in the former than the latter field. Dr. Knorr, friend and counselor to scores of faculty and graduates at the University, contributes a first-class scholarly and scientific review of physical illness and resulting psychological functions, alcoholism, psychological disorders, dementia, personality disorders, anesthesia as well as an overview of his subject. In effect, Dr. Knorr and Harrington have given the present study commission and commissions to follow a working document of measurable scientific validity. They have filled a gap in knowledge of which the Miller Center Commission in its early studies was acutely aware. They have brought the best available scientific knowledge to the public affairs marketplace.

Professor James Childress, who is the current chairman of the Department of Religious Studies, is an authority on bio-medical ethics. Within that sphere of competence, he has concerned himself with confidentiality in physician-patient relationships. That issue proved a puzzle and a

xi

recurrent subject for debate within the commission. To what extent can a presidential physician breach confidence if the national security is in jeopardy? In a highly original and rigorous analytical study, Dr. Childress draws important distinctions that any physician must weigh in departing, even in limited ways, from confidentiality. His paper also provides the kind of guidelines the Commission sought throughout its study on emergent issues. It is a model of ethical evaluation by a leading American ethicist. Appropriately, Childress brings the Miller Center inquiry to a close with this discussion.

THE TWENTY-FIFTH AMENDMENT:

ITS HISTORY AND MEANING

Senator Birch E. Bayh, Jr.

NARRATOR: We've thought of presidential disability as your bailiwick, Senator Bayh. We've wanted to consult with you about it before we got very far into the subject. As you know, the Miller Center overall is trying to do two things. One is to study the presidency and the second is to make some moves in the direction of improving or acting with others to improve certain aspects of the presidency. That was the will of the donor who established the Center and we've tried to be faithful to his wishes. The other commissions that we've organized include one on the presidency and the press, another on the nominating process and one on presidential transitions and foreign policy. The whole area of presidential disability seemed to be another fundamental, vital and crucial area.

When we heard you discussing the way in which the Twenty-fifth Amendment was not formally invoked, and yet in practice was invoked, when you were interviewed on television during the President's cancer surgery, it brought to mind that you obviously were the person at the center of all this when the legislation was written and had perhaps the clearest view of it all. I wonder if it would be useful to begin our deliberations by asking if you would revisit the legislation and deliberations that led to Twenty-fifth Amendment and then say anything you might want to say that would help us zero in on what we ought to be thinking about in this whole sphere. It would be very helpful if you would kick off and then I think others around the table will certainly have questions.

1

SENATOR BAYH: I'll be happy to follow any lead. I couldn't help but notice this very nice brochure in which you cite the mandate of the Center—"the underlying concern is how to reconcile a need for effective central leadership with the constitutional provisions for limited government with divided but shared power, particularly under domestic and world conditions of the late twentieth century." That pretty well summarizes what we were trying to come up grips with in the Twenty-fifth Amendment.

I suppose when we first got started, the biggest obstacle we had to overcome was the fact that we had almost two hundred years of history in which there had never been a president and a vice president die during one four-year period. There is a good deal of status quo thinking in the Senate, as in the old cliche, "If it ain't broke, don't fix it." That was one thing we had to overcome. We had been confronted with a number of presidential illnesses and disabilities—Garfield, Wilson, Eisenhower, and, of course, some of more recent vintage. We had, I think, eight presidents die; seven vice presidents die; and John C. Calhoun resigned to go back to South Carolina and run for the Senate. So there were sixteen instances in which we had no vice president for one reason or another, but never had we lost both in the same four years. As it turned out, almost before the ink was dry on all the documents, we were confronted with some very unfortunate circumstances which caused the first part, the succession part of the Amendment, to be used and I think it probably served the country very well. I can't believe in my heart of hearts that Richard Nixon would have ever resigned and turned the power of the presidency over to Carl Albert, so the country would have been dragged through a rather dramatic impeachment trial. I think it worked pretty well when Jerry Ford filled the successor's role under a portion of the Twenty-fifth Amendment.

We were trying to separate and deal with the two different problems. One of the problems we had was the fact that this was an area that had not received a great deal of study. A senator or congressman or any person who's actively involved in the political process who starts an objective study of presidential disability or the possibility that the president or vice president might die when neither one of them are ill, is immediately suspect. When you are confronted with illness or death, then circumstances change so quickly that it is almost too late to study presidential succession in an objective way. The personalities and circumstances of the moment govern the response instead of enabling decision-makers to sit back and have a detached view of how to approach the situation. As tragic as the Kennedy assassination was, it gave the opportunity to begin looking at the succession problem at a time when nobody could question your motivation. I recall riding back from a meeting in Atlantic City, New Jersey with Lyndon Johnson in his chopper. I thought this would be a good chance to lobby him a little bit for his support on this amendment which, by then, we had gotten passed through the Senate. This was about mid-1964. It was his accurate judgment that we wouldn't get anything passed until after the election. Once we had a sitting vice president, it would not be considered an affront to Speaker Carl Albert. Basically, that was the chronology of the situation when we came back a second time and we did get it through in relatively short order.

Let me think out loud about *succession*, which is not as difficult a problem as that of *disability*. You have more time to act even if you don't have a vice president. The country has someone in total and complete control with the authority of the presidency. So, you have a little more time to act and make a reasoned judgment on what should be done to fill the vice presidential vacancy.

The thing that came through is that there is nothing quite like presidential power. Some people will almost kill to get it and some will almost kill to keep it. Historically, this becomes a larger problem when you get into the disability discussion—the question is not so much a medical question as a political one. In looking at the question of how to fill a vacancy, there are all sorts of things to look at—special elections and various methods of appointment. It seemed to us we needed to accomplish two things.

First, we needed to have a vice president who could work in harmony with the president. Historically, we've had some sad instances where the president and the vice president were at war with one another. Certainly, in a time of crisis when you have a death in one of those

3

offices and you are trying to fill the resulting vacancy in the vice presidency, the last thing you want to do is to put someone in there who becomes a constant source of friction.

It is also important to consider the fact that the vice presidential office has grown and has been given additional responsibilities not granted before, to help share some of the burdens of the presidency. But that maturation of the vice presidential office accomplishes nothing if the president doesn't trust the vice president. He is not going to give and delegate any authority to him if he doesn't trust him.

We thought the one thing we really needed to have would be someone whom the president could feel confident about and could trust. We didn't want to have an anointment, an heir apparent that could be chosen by the incumbent president. There had to be some sort of democratization of the process—other than a special election in which someone could be elected who was not the president's choice and who might not be harmonious with the president. We thought that Congress, sitting as sort of a revised electoral college, with each state having the same weight as on the electoral college would be best. Those people are supposed to know a lot about public policy and usually they do. Perhaps more importantly than anything else, we thought a congressional choice or ratification was something that would be accepted by the people. If something happened to the president, and the newly chosen vice president succeeded to the president, there would not be a question about the authority of this individual to actually go ahead and serve. So we had the president nominate and the Congress confirm.

In terms of thoughts that went through our minds at the time, we wanted, as closely as possible, to approximate a choice that would have been made by the people at the time of the election. That is not always easy to do. But, since we weren't having a special election, I thought that this was something we really owed to the people—not to make independent judgments but to try to accept the president's will if we thought the person was qualified and if we thought the people would have made a similar choice.

That's why I found myself in a rather interesting and difficult situation. I was asked to be the first witness at the time Jerry Ford was nominated by the President. It was my judgment that Congressman Ford was clearly within the guidelines that we anticipated when we passed the Twenty-fifth Amendment. The President had trust in him. His philosophy was consistent with the environment that existed at the time President Nixon was elected. I did not feel the same way when President Ford recommended Vice President Rockefeller. I thought he was not the type of person that would have been chosen by the people at the same time they were electing President Nixon, although I personally would have preferred Rockefeller to Nixon as president. Members of Congress had to make that decision for themselves. It certainly put me in a rather difficult, and what might have seemed inconsistent, position. But I thought I had good grounds for looking at one one way and one the other.

QUESTION: Were you a witness on that, too?

SENATOR BAYH: No. I wasn't. The situation that existed was that the Republican party had consistently turned down Nelson Rockefeller. We were, at that particular moment, very much involved in the throes of the oil crisis and with the Rockefeller background in that sphere, I thought the people would be concerned if the events required him to ascend to the presidency. What he did as vice president was really not what concerned me, but the question you had to look at was whether this person is qualified and how he is going to be accepted if he gets to be president.

The disability question is a much more difficult question. Crass as it may sound, I think it is true that it is much easier to deal with the disposition of presidential power when a president is dead, or if no one is in the office of vice president, than it is to try to determine what to do when the person who is elected and chosen as president is disabled and alive, but unable to perform the duties of the office. It is not only a question of what to do, but when to do it, who makes the determination and what to do if he recovers. Real concern was raised about whether a law could deal with the question of how to get the power back to the president once someone else had exercised it. In the Twenty-fifth Amendment, we talk about the vice president having the power and duties but not actually being the president as long as the president himself is alive.

There were many well-intentioned and reasonable alternatives proposed—a blue ribbon panel involving the Supreme Court, chief justice, congressional leaders, doctors and lawyers of various titles, all competent individuals. I didn't feel that we could ignore the fact that this was as much a political question as a medical one. We tried to make it as easy to use the amendment as possible.

Historically, we had found a great reluctance to come to grips with the fact that a president was ill. Former President Nixon probably the most dramatic witness we had, was our last witness and he was the person who described what it was like to be vice president when President Eisenhower was under an oxygen tent. Suddenly, there you are. Fortunately we were not confronted then with missiles in Cuba or something that needed immediate attention. But it seemed to me that what we needed to have was a system which was as easy as possible to implement and in which there was the least amount of room for mischief; a mechanism that would insure that there would always be continuity in the utilization of those powers and duties of the president.

The recent use of the Twenty-fifth Amendment, described as a non-use by President Reagan, was exactly the kind of thing we had in mind. When Wilson or Garfield was disabled the possibility of destroying the world while a president was unconscious was not a real possibility. Now civilization as we know it can be destroyed in a matter of minutes. It is important for the country and our allies and adversaries to know that there is no hiatus. Even if it is only for thirty minutes or an hour or three hours, there needs to be a system in which the vice president is given the power to act in the event of unforeseen emergencies. We came up with a provision which permitted the president to voluntarily give up the powers and almost immediately take them back. It seemed to us that was the surest way to guarantee the system would be used. If the president is going to be under anesthesia, why shouldn't he, as President Reagan did, turn his powers and duties over to the vice president? The fact that Vice President Bush was not acting president very long doesn't mean that it didn't work. It means that it did work.

QUESTION: I wonder if you could pause right here and analyze the letter that passed between the President and Vice President. What do you make of that letter and why was it drafted that way?

SENATOR BAYH: Obviously, I was not privileged to any inside information. Nobody from the White House called me. I don't know of anybody else they called to ask what Congress meant. It seems to me they should have asked what we were really after. I can imagine that they had made a conscious determination, which they thought correct, that this was not going to be serious enough to worry about. It was going to be a brief period of unconsciousness. One has to understand that whenever something like this is utilized, there is a good possibility that the leader's unconscious state will be dramatized and the public may over-react. There was concern about the impact on the stock market. You could make a good case for not wanting to over-dramatize it. But it seemed to me that the best way not to over-dramatize it was to say, "This isn't anything special, it is only what the Constitution requires. This is not a big deal; it is not serious. We're just doing what is required by the Constitution. The President is going to take powers back as soon as he is well." For the most part, that is what they did.

But they made a much bigger issue out of it. If I had to bet the farm, which I wouldn't, I think that when they were confronted by that nine o'clock press conference and Sam Donaldson and some of the rest of them started asking questions for which there were no good answers, they had a quick session with some of the people around the President. They decided they had to do something. They said if our refusal to use the Twenty-fifth Amendment is going to be blown out of all proportion, let's go ahead and find a way to use it. So somebody was given the task of putting something together that was a use/non-use proposition. I think it was poorly drafted. Rather than saying we don't want to establish a precedent, they should have recognized that no president is going to use what his predecessor has done unless he feels it's a good precedent. This was the time for a good precedent to be set. I have to believe that any presidential staff, if it had time to thoroughly go over the proposed letter, would have seen all of the shortcomings that existed in that piece of paper. So, I believe it was just a quick decision drafted as the President was on his way to the operating room. Be that as it may, it worked well and nobody was any worse for it.

QUESTION: I would disagree that the President was ready to come back. If you take a seventy-four year old person and put him under major surgery and follow that with narcotics, I don't want him in charge of the "football." Eight hours after major surgery he said he was ready to assume the duties and powers of the office. That's baloney! One of the weaknesses is letting the president himself decide when he's ready to come back.

SENATOR BAYH: I think medically you are absolutely right. I would ask: "You know what people are like post-operative. How can anyone say the President is alert and ready to function?" My only point is, is there any other mechanism other than the president himself saying he is ready to come back?

QUESTION: What about the presidential physician? Was that ever considered?

SENATOR BAYH: Yes. Not only was that considered but it is available in another provision of the Twenty-fifth Amendment. If I had been there, I probably would have said, "What's the rush?" There was no real reason for him to rush back into power, except I think there was a feeling within the administration that something had to be done quickly to let the country know that it was not a serious problem. So they rushed it and that was medically premature. You have to weigh that against the politics. If you are setting up a mechanism to transfer presidential power, there will be a certain paranoia among the palace guard in the White House. That has to be at least one of the reasons there have been such major confrontations between presidents and vice presidents. Any little thing

8

that the vice president does is considered encroachment or a threat to the throne. Look at the situation that existed at George Washington University Hospital. When the President was shot, there seemed as good a reason if not a better one to use the Twenty-fifth Amendment. But it wasn't used.

You had Secretary of State Haig in the White House saying that everything's under control. Frankly, I thought he was criticized unnecessarily. He did perform a service as far as our allies and adversaries are concerned. The real problem was that you had Haig in the White House saying one thing and Meese and Baker at George Washington saying another. You had a President who might have been able to whisper or to communicate to Baker and Meese and they were the ones that were closest to knowing the President's will, not Haig. It did not become the kind of an issue you had under Wilson, with the secretary of state calling cabinet meetings because nothing else could be done. He was canned for being disloyal as soon as the President had the mental capacity to make any decisions. You didn't have that kind of situation.

It seemed to me and to all of us in drafting the amendment, that it was worth the premature reclaiming possibility, on the one hand, in order to get the implementation of the disability provisions, on the other. But you have a President surrounded by people that say, "Mr. President, you can't trust so and so. You don't know what he's going to do if you're unconscious and we know that you are capable and you know what George Bush tried to do to you at that convention and in New Hampshire, and what he said about you. You just can't trust those folks."

Let's put your question to rest by saying that if the president really is going to be out of it, at least he is going to recognize that and hopefully will be able to make a considered judgment as to whether he should be in control. If a president feels that he has to go before a medical board or a group of "wise men" (and wisdom is often in the eyes of the beholder, particularly if you are president), there is going to be great reluctance to give up that power in the first place.

9

QUESTION: Your comment about paranoia and the vice presidency leads me to one of my main questions. In light of that, what was the reasoning in Section 4 for involving the vice president? He's an essential cog under Section 4; you can't take any action in Section 4 without the vice president concurring. It seems to me that your point cuts against involving the vice president at all, because he's always seen as a lurking potential threat anyway.

SENATOR BAYH: It does not do any good to have a provision unless the people who are going to play the game are willing to suit up and go out on the field. We didn't want a John Marshall hiding under the bed someplace saying that even if Mrs. Wilson asks me, I'm not going to accept the responsibility. If the Constitution says, "Mr. Vice President, you are supposed to act," it seemed to us that there was a better chance of getting him actually to act and accept the responsibilities. It's not something he does because he is power hungry. He does it because that's what the Constitution says he should do.

That presents a series of vexatious questions and I guess all of us have to be a little paranoid about presidential *coup d'etats* and efforts to get that power that are not really in the national interest. We tried to protect the president from a malicious vice president intent on seizing power for himself prematurely by giving the president the protection of his own Cabinet.

It was literally after 11:00 a.m. one night and before we finally passed this provision, that I suddenly sensed that things were falling apart. We had Gene McCarthy, Phil Hart, Bobby Kennedy and two or three others in the cloak room of the Senate and Bobby Kennedy was raising reservations about this problem. I went back to project myself into the discussion and Bobby turned to me and said, "Birch, don't you realize that President Kennedy didn't know any of the members of his cabinet personally until he appointed them? They were not people who had been members of the family." Well, obviously, he did know them. But he didn't know them well. It was Bobby's feeling that they were not the kind of people who could be trusted to protect the President as Bobby defined the necessity of protecting the President. But I've got to believe that

10

anybody who has been appointed and served on a presidential cabinet has enough loyalty that they are going to be loyal to the president until it is not in the national interest to do so. At that stage of the game it is not a question of personal loyalty. It is a question of doing what's right for the country. We were not oblivious to the fact that you might have a situation like the Wilson one in which cabinet members began to talk about the need to do something yet did not act despite the obvious inability of the President. That's why we provided for the case of a cabinet's dilatory refusal to exercise the powers of the Twenty-fifth Amendment. In this event, the Congress, recognizing the situation, can establish another body of "wise men" or medical experts or some other group to serve as a panel to look at the disability question in a more objective way.

QUESTION: On that point, was this "such other group that Congress may by law enact" put in there only for a kind of a backup emergency situation if Congress saw that the cabinet wasn't acting?

In other words, did you contemplate that Congress would enact a general statute in the future substituting another body for the cabinet? Or was it more of an emergency fail-safe kind of provision?

SENATOR BAYH: We thought of it in both perspectives. First, it was designed for an emergency situation which would call to everyone's attention the fact that the present system wasn't working, at least at that particular time. The Amendment is designed so that Congress can create a different vehicle. We were concerned about the politics of the palace *coup*. So in reality, we created a vehicle where it is more difficult to declare a president disabled than it is to impeach him for a breach of his constitutional duties. Maybe we went too far but I don't necessarily think so. I am confident that if it had just taken a majority of the Congress, that Andrew Johnson wouldn't have been impeached, but he would have been driven out of office as being unable to perform physically and mentally. What we were trying to do was to create an instrument that would permit all the players to act in a

11

manner that would be acceptable to the public and prevent a breakdown of faith in governmental institutions.

QUESTION: Senator, if I could follow-up on the previous question, do you think that if Congress were to create some other body, such as you've been talking about, is it your understanding that the veto power would apply or not?

SENATOR BAYH: Yes.

QUESTION: Following up on that, is it your view that under the Twenty-fifth Amendment, coupled with the "necessary and proper" clause, that Congress could enact a statute that would describe certain procedures or steps to be followed by the vice president and the cabinet or the other body that it might create? How far can Congress go in spelling out the mechanics or procedures that those players must follow in order to write a decision about disability?

SENATOR BAYH: I think they could pass an act that would provide for procedures. They could establish a procedural format to be followed. What we were trying to do was find a way which would meet with public acceptance, and then understanding by public officials, that the public would accept it, would be willing to utilize it. In short, we wanted to find a way in which presidential disability would not become a matter of leprosy. Presidents get ill. That's particularly why we had the provision that was used by President Reagan. If a president recognizes he is ill and the people recognize that presidents become ill, it becomes less a major consequence when it happens. The stock market doesn't gyrate. It's a matter of business as usual, which is the way I wished that President Reagan had approached this. I think that is a sure way of lessening public reaction or concern.

QUESTION: Was there any discussion of a substitute for the vice president at this early stage when somebody calls on Congress in this twenty-one day process to consider action? One proposal suggested in a preliminary discussion we had was that some very trusted figure other than the vice president, thus avoiding the problem of vice president being judge and jury, might call on the Congress to consider it. It would be a distinguished person such as the chief justice or somebody else. Was that ever considered? Or was the vice president in these early stages always looked on as the natural person to initiate it?

SENATOR BAYH: The vice president was always under consideration, but not the only person under consideration. The Supreme Court, I think it was Justice Warren, did not look favorably on a role for the Supreme Court in a situation like that.

COMMENT: Neither does Warren Burger.

SENATOR BAYH: It seemed to be a separation of powers question. In the final analysis, I guess one could structure a scenario in which the Supreme Court has a role.

What we were trying to do was to find a way, imperfect as it is, to recognize this for what it really is. It is a matter in which public people, politicians and government officials, are the players and they are the ones that are going to have to carry out the decisions. So, perhaps they ought to be in on the decision-making process as it proceeds.

Most of the concern in the discussions as I recall them, was to protect the president from an overly zealous vice president wanting to assume the role of president. History shows us, and probably common sense as well, that the vice president has been very reluctant to act and it doesn't do us any good to put the vice president in a role unless he is willing to accept that role. We thought by including him in the process at the beginning, you would have less of a John Marshall situation. The vice president would be more willing to go ahead and say, "All right, this is what the Constitution suggests I do and I'm prepared to do it, and present it to the cabinet for their approval. If they don't approve, then all right, I'm still the vice president and we'll hope the president gets well quickly."

There are three separate circumstances, although there is some overlapping. In one, you have a president who is in full control of his capacities and makes an educated, thoughtful determination that it is in the best interest of everyone for him to voluntarily turn over the powers of duties. The second set of circumstances is designed to deal with a president who is unexpectedly struck down; for example, Eisenhower in the oxygen tent or a president who is suddenly no longer able to perform. Then what do you do? In the real world, probably what you would do is nothing, for a period of time anyhow, until the vice president has a chance to consult with a lot of folks as to whether something needs to be done. You have the informal agreements that have been passed on from one generation of presidents and vice presidents to subsequent ones that provide some protection there. It could be that as long as those are working properly and there is no emergency, maybe there would be no official act on the part of this vice president and the cabinet.

COMMENT: That was the assassination model, wasn't it? We were told, for instance, that it all happened too fast. They really had not thought through what they should do. This is what Dr. Ruge said. They weren't ready at that time. I don't know if that is something that politicians would tell you. That is, Meese and Baker might have told you something else. But by the time of the surgery we were told they did know they had to do something and they had documents in place.

SENATOR BAYH: It is only natural, I assume, that people around the president would think in terms of a president who was shot, killed, or almost killed. However, it would be unwise if that were the only contingency that they plan for. It is a difficult thing to sit down and talk with the president of the United States and say, "Mr. President, you know somebody might shoot you or you might have a heart attack." That's a very difficult kind of thing to discuss, but I think it should be discussed. I thought, starting with Eisenhower, that had been a matter that had been discussed at the beginning of each administration, but apparently it was not the case.

QUESTION: Since the adoption of the Twenty-fifth Amendment, has anything happened in the country, that is

14

to say, have any circumstances changed in your view? I refer to circumstances relating to the way the White House is organized, the White House staff, the nature of procedures in the White House, or any other events and circumstances since the members adopted it that would cause you to now wonder whether the Amendment might be drafted somewhat differently if you had to do it today in light of what we now know?

SENATOR BAYH: Not to my knowledge. For any structure that you create, you can always envision a scenario in which certain players go off half-cocked or are poorly motivated and cause it to malfunction and to reach consequences that none of us would like to see happen. I think what we tried to do is to set up a system that would work generally with people of good will. I think it was Senator Everett Dirksen who said it well. At one session he said when the nation is confronted with a crisis you have to assume that people of good will are going to do the right thing and that's where you get into the third scenario. First, you give it up voluntarily; second, it's an instantaneous striking down of a president; and third, you have a president alive and walking and talking, but not well. That is the mental illness question which is really the most difficult one to deal with. That is where you can structure all sorts of scenarios of what might happen but you have to reach down and rely on men and women of good faith doing what's in the country's interest in that situation.

I must confess that if one looks at the consideration process of the House Judiciary Committee during the Nixon impeachment hearings, I find myself a little more comfortable with the scenario we've structured after seeing how Republicans and Democrats alike responded. I think what each person did was in the best interest of the country, not necessarily their party or themselves personally. But I think it's a good example of how democratic institutions ought to function. They don't always function that way. Maybe I'm being too naive, but historically people tend to rise to the level needed to serve the nation.

15

QUESTION: Before we get to the mental illness topic, may I ask whether one possible tension was ever discussed? We've been struck by the fact—listening to the Arthur Miller/Fred Friendly type program—that one group thought the White House should play a determining role. Basically, that group considers that they are closest to the President. The White House staff sees him all the time and knows what he can do. There was almost a sense of resentment that somebody else would substitute for White House aides in the judgment. Don Regan, after all, took over to a very considerable degree and the argument was that he and Nancy Reagan were talking and he was closer to the scene than the vice president.

Another group that seems to feel that they are not given the role that professionally they think they should have are the doctors. Dr. Ruge referred to the fact that the president's personal physician is "a blue collar job" under present circumstances. He didn't ever appear before the cabinet and they didn't ask him his advice. There seems to be a slight quirk in the picture in the reaction of these two groups. The White House physicians and the White House staff feel they ought to have a special role as they see it and they aren't given as much responsibility as they think they ought to have. Were these two groups considered at all as to what they ought to do and have a right to do when you talked about it?

SENATOR BAYH: Yes. They were considered. Here again we are operating without a great deal of empirical evidence. We have a select set of circumstances. Every example we have so far of how White House staffs respond does not recommend that they or presidential wives ought to be able to determine this matter. Without being critical of presidential wives, they act as wives instead of first ladies; they want to protect their husbands. It's not that they are disloyal but a normal reaction of a woman or a man is to want to protect his or her spouse and not really to be able to comprehend the dramatic impact that those personal decisions have on the well-being of the country. I don't think that Mrs. Wilson intentionally set out to create a situation where we would have more problems because she sheltered the President, but that was the consequence.

16

I think White House staff should be considered. They should be given an opportunity to be heard, but honestly I wonder. This is, after all, the first time this provision was used. I sensed that once that vehicle had been used the first time, there was not going to be the reservations about going ahead and using it the second time. Maybe now that it has been used once, even though it wasn't used according to the letter, it may be used better the second time. If one looks at the situation, it is relatively easy to make a determination of whether the president is going to be able to respond or not. If he's going to be unconscious, he's not going to be able to respond and so we ought to be able to make that judgment.

The second question is why rush to take power back and that is a good question. I think they rushed too quickly to take it back. It made little sense with a sedated President. But they were well intentioned. They thought this would allay public fear. With the third category where the question of a president's ability to perform is being contested, then you have some time. Congress is sitting in judgment. You bring in the medical experts and constitutional authorities and that gives you the opportunity to examine the particular kind of illness in the abstract and also to talk to the specific physicians that are dealing with the specific case. You can come to a more learned decision than would normally be the case.

QUESTION: Under Section 3 you would think that a president would be able to identify his own disability, such as undergoing surgery and receiving anesthesia, and would be able himself to invoke Section 3 of the Amendment in a very straightforward manner recognizing that he's going to be out of it and that the vice president will be in charge. The public would support that and there wouldn't be any great anxiety. But it seems that the president and his family and those around the president are the ones that are most upset or troubled and it may be more than just the palace revolt with the vice president. Some fear the president would be perceived as weak and incapable, which he certainly would be under anesthesia. However the persons around the president, including his family, try to deny that he will be disabled. We see this phenomenon in hospital

17

rooms all the time when someone is in a coma, the mother or daughter or someone will say, "I think he recognized my voice because I saw his eyes move." Maybe that is where the work should be done with the president and those around him. You would say, look, this is matter of fact, you have to invoke the amendment. It is a part of the Constitution. Don't be concerned about the public. They are going to understand your being under anesthesia and not being capable for a period of time. Encourage discussions or some interaction among the president and his cabinet, his staff, his family, to take the pressure off because they must feel very threatened. I think it's more than just what could happen or what kind of mischief the vice president could get into.

SENATOR BAYH: I do not know if it is the drinking water at the White House or what it is, but there is an environment down there (and I don't think any of us fully appreciate it unless we've had a chance to work outside the president's door) that affects everybody that is submerged in that environment. There is a tenacious desire to hold on to presidential power and not to trust other people with it. I think the President botched it. Invoking the amendment would have been in his own interest. There is a great deal of sympathy politically. I think the people rally around someone who says, "I'm ill" and then does what is necessary to protect the country. He might say: "I'm going to do A, B, C, and D, and then I'm going to be well again and we're going to go on and we're going to do what we set out to do." I think there is a rush to support a president like that. I think it is to the credit of the press and the journalists, some of whom are very close allies of the President, that writers like Bill Safire were analytically very critical of what happened. That might increase the chances that it will be done right the next time.

QUESTION: It seems to me that one of the troubling things is that we can be twenty-nine days without an acting president—with no one in charge of the football. My question is, was the provision of four days in which the president could come back and say, " I'm all right," was that to prevent a *coup*? The vice president initiates it with the cabinet and, if I interpret it correctly, the president can say, "You're wrong; I'm okay." And the president has four days to do that. Isn't that right? Is that to prevent a *coup*?

SENATOR BAYH: That's to permit some time to deliberate before making that decision because the president himself needs to be aware that there are going to be people who are going to disagree with him on that. Then maybe he'll go back and have a conversation with his doctors and say, "Am I really well?" Or he may talk to his lawyers and other people to see what he is really getting himself involved in if he is determined to go ahead and do it. The fact of the matter is, since we are probably talking about mental illness here, that the time-frame probably won't dissuade the president. But we thought there ought to be some time to let him have a chance to consider all the contingencies.

QUESTION: Why did you give Congress twenty-one days? To get back to Washington?

SENATOR BAYH: That was half-way between the time the House wanted and the time the Senate wanted.

QUESTION: In a real emergency twenty-one days is a long time, isn't it, in the era of the football?

SENATOR BAYH: Yes. At that stage of the game you have to decide whether it is better to have the president or the vice president acting. Both of them have been elected by the people. One of them has just been disabled. Is it more likely that the nation will be served in the same capacity by someone who hasn't been disabled than by someone who has been disabled during that time-frame? It was our judgment that we would, given all the circumstances, have the vice president with the majority of the president's cabinet and his own cabinet functioning during that period while the president's sanity was being decided. I hope our country is never confronted with that kind of situation. Of course, you could have a raving lunatic and I think that would be dealt with pretty quickly, but there is the possibility of someone who could be very ill mentally but smart enough to know how to act.

QUESTION: Could he contest it? Could he in any way challenge the twenty-one days?

COMMENT: He could come back every four days, couldn't he? In the Constitution it doesn't say how many times a president can challenge the action.

SENATOR BAYH: Yes, but I think to the extent he does that the second time he's going to lose by a larger vote than the first time.

What we are trying to say is that we don't care whether it is the president or the vice president that is active. You don't know who the players will be, but we feel that the formula was such that the country would be better served if you had the continuity of someone who had been consistently able to perform rather than having someone rush back in who had been unable to perform and suddenly reclaim the powers. The country would be better served by having the vice president in that period. Here again, the vice president would be reinforced by the president's cabinet which we thought was ample protection during that twenty-one day period until the Congress could decide.

I must confess I am not completely comfortable with what would be going on in Congress during a debate like that. That is a horrible situation to try to envisage. But it is the least undesirable of any other alternative. I don't know how else you could have it done. You can't have an election in a situation like that.

QUESTION: Would there be a public debate in Congress?

SENATOR BAYH: Oh yes, there would be a public debate. As I said a moment ago, I think you would call witnesses. Certainly, the cabinet and the vice president would all want to have as many medical witnesses as possible to show why their actions were well founded. The president, on the other hand, would want to try and get people to support his contentions. So, I think the public would have a pretty good feel for what was being done. Here, again, I am comforted in my reservation about the terrible nature of that kind of a dialogue by what happened in the House Judiciary Committee during the impeachment hearings.

QUESTION: Assuming that the Twenty-fifth Amendment stands as it is, do you have any thoughts or any ideas about legislation Congress might enact that would help the situation at all? Is there something Congress could do given the existence of the Twenty-fifth Amendment? Is there any legislation that might smooth it out a bit or help in any way?

SENATOR BAYH: I hadn't thought about that for a long time until my phone started ringing the Friday before the Saturday operation on President Reagan. Suddenly I started revisiting the question. I think anything that Congress can do to make the utilization of the Twenty-fifth Amendment appear to be sort of like reading the morning paper—the accepted thing to do and not a matter that should send shock waves through the country or the world—would be a positive thing. I have to say, unless things have changed significantly since I was in the Senate, the possibility of getting someone to run with that is not great. If you had a president who was determined to do something and leads the charge—if you have President Reagan and the White House palace guard that has gone through this and now think there are other things that should be put in the statute that would help them make a decision earlier or help provide support for a decision—I think you'd have congressional acceptance. You would need presidential leadership. Other than that, I fear that people are going to be fearful that their motives would be challenged.

QUESTION: Could I ask Dan Meador a question on that? You got the impression that both Mr. Meese and Mr. Fielding, and more particularly people working with Mr. Fielding, would not discourage an outside group (indeed to some extent, they would encourage an outside group) from looking at this subject. Did they give any indication of any area in which, following Senator Bayh's suggestion, they might, if they had freedom to act, want to provide some additional statutory provisions?

PROFESSOR MEADOR: No, I did not get any impression one way or the other on that point. I think the most I got out of these conversations was that they would not be opposed to some independent commission studying the whole thing. In other words, I got no sense that they have suggestions about specific legislation or any other steps beyond simply a study by some group. There was a sense that it probably would have to be an independent body, that Congress is unlikely to touch it on its own initiative. You are not likely to get any White House attention or any serious Justice Department efforts in any open way. It's just a hot potato and any way you move on it in government is likely to be misconstrued by somebody.

SENATOR BAYH: The American Bar Association gave us an opportunity to study this without anybody really questioning our motives as would otherwise have been the case. I think an independent group, perhaps a Miller Center Commission, given its impressive credentials, would help. But, I wonder Dan, can you envision a White House staff person who would respond to your question, "No, I don't want anybody poking around in it; that's our business."

It would certainly be in the national interest if everybody who had gone through this kind of situation would really 'fess up. There is nothing to hide. We are talking about things that happen to families every day. In this case, it's the first family and so it makes it a different kind of situation, but I think the fear that the public reaction would be bad is not well founded.

QUESTION: If you felt that the president was quietly psychotic or had some cerebral deficit because of, say, early Alzheimer's disease and you as a private citizen felt that this was a great danger to the nation, who would you go to or how would you, as a private citizen, take action? Right now I think you would have to go to the Cabinet or the vice president.

SENATOR BAYH: I don't see how any lay person can proceed in a manner that would be credible. Armed with probably more than one opinion—and you would want substantiating opinions—I think the place I would go would probably be to somebody like Senator Strom Thurmond, chairman of the Senate Judiciary Committee and a member of the President's own party. To deal with the politics of the situation you pretty well have to enlist the support and concurrence of someone of the president's own party in order for it not to look like it is politically motivated.

QUESTION: Then that person could follow up? Where would Strom Thurmond go? What would he do in order to begin this Twenty-fifth Amendment process?

SENATOR BAYH: Strom may or may not be a good example. So much depends on what personal relationships each individual has. If you have a personal relationship with somebody in the White House, you might go there. The reason I think it is important to get someone within the Congress enlisted is that if it were someone who had a political background such as mine who were to go in unsupported, nobody would listen. If you enlist someone from Congress and if you enlist medical professionals, then Congress has a role to play. People in the Cabinet or at the White House might conclude that they had better do something or Congress might feel inclined to get involved, although the Twenty-fifth Amendment does not permit Congress to initiate it.

COMMENT: I guess that is the point. If the president came on television and said, "This is Easter Monday and we're in great danger from some foreign power," you could get more attention, but unless you go directly to the Cabinet and the vice president to invoke Section 4 you have quite a problem. And there you are dealing with people who have a tremendous conflict of interest.

SENATOR BAYH: If you had a Thurmond or turned to a Dole or someone so that you could develop a consensus, at least you would have more than one person. You could organize a small cadre of people that then can go to the

Executive Branch and say we've got trouble here and we think the country needs to be alerted. I don't think you can go directly to the vice president because he is not going to entertain that idea unsupported. Thinking in terms of political values, if you go to the vice president and you have the attorney general of the United States with you, or the secretary of state or secretary of defense, then the vice president—who may have been suspicious of this all along and didn't know what to do about it—can at least entertain the idea without others suspecting that he's angling for the president's office.

Suppose you had a president and every time he had a press conference, he had to have another press conference explaining what he had said in the first one. We've had a lot of second-guessing going on and many little snafus with the present President, but I don't think that is serious enough that anybody feels that they should move in on the President. But how do you determine mental illness? That is a tough question.

QUESTION: How do you avoid mistaking rumors and signals, for instance, Nixon's drinking or the Louisville Debate? Do you have to have a succession of things that prove or disprove what we're told in the public? Must there be hard evidence on the medical side? Whom do you believe when Haig says he's running the government because the President can't run it? We've had several people who have said that Haig specialized from time to time in this kind of leaking and planting rumors around the White House. How can you get medical judgments on any of these things?

COMMENT: If you come back to a previous question, the person closest to Roosevelt outside of the Cabinet was Jim Farley and he was absolutely right when he said in 1943 that the President was sick. He went to John Nance Garner and Garner said, "Boy, forget it!" It was merely interpreted by the press that Farley wanted to be president—which he did. So I don't know that even people close to the president will initiate that.

COMMENT: The person that would be most likely to do it or most competent historically is the president's physician.

Wilson had a physician that helped prop him up in the last sixteen months of the presidency. Roosevelt's physician diagnosed and covered up for the President and I think the same is true for Kennedy with his Addison's disease. So when you talk about an objective observer from the medical field, I don't know where you are going to find one just by the nature of the doctor/patient relationship. Any physician is going to know his patient well, especially the president, and is going to develop all sorts of ties to that person. It's going to be very difficult to ask the president to step down, much less go behind the president's back and inform the vice president or Congress.

COMMENT: I think Doctor Ruge indicated where he would go should he observe unusual behavior and feel there was serious mental disorder. I believe he said he would go to the attorney general.

COMMENT: But he said he would go to the president first.

COMMENT: Yes, he certainly did. He said that was his responsibility.

SENATOR BAYH: Everything we've said here is absolutely true in terms of the difficulties inherent in the loyalty factor. The first person that ought to be able to determine illness is the president's spouse or the president's doctor. I don't think there is anything you can put in the Constitution or that you could put in the statute that can suddenly change human nature. Perhaps this is wishful thinking, but I believe that as this vehicle is used, slowly but surely you will begin to find public acceptance. I would think that perhaps a wife who really knew her husband was dramatically ill and that the burdens of the presidency were killing him might be inclined to do this or to at least say, "Well, Woodrow, let's have a little rest."

COMMENT: Do you know what Wilson told her and Admiral Grayson? He said it would kill him if he had to resign and furthermore Grayson told him to run again because it would make him feel better.

QUESTION: Let me ask this question. Do you have any view at the moment as to what, if anything useful, an independent study commission could contribute? Are there particular segments of the problem which could usefully be addressed or any sort of recommendations that might be made? Is it worth a lot of hard study by some independent group right now?

SENATOR BAYH: I don't know how to answer that last question but I think the answer to the first question is, yes. I think a contribution could be made. Perhaps there are ways in which the verbiage of the Amendment itself or corroborating, supporting or even delicately revised statutory language could be helpful. But I wonder if, from a practical standpoint, the largest contribution wouldn't be public awareness and thus presidential awareness. It would have to be handled so that it would not be viewed as critical of the way the administration handled this the last time. Instead, perhaps what is said could be complimentary of the fact that this was done for the first time, but the next time, since it has been done once, it would be better to do it this way. I think the extent that the public and political people—the next White House chief of staff—is aware of this, it is a good thing. Maybe the next time the White House will give different advice to the commander in chief or the next president himself will be made better aware of what the options are. When I was first called on the telephone to be on the David Brinkley show on Sunday, it was designed to be a criticism of the president's not using it. They said, don't you think he should use it; won't you come on the program and let us interview you for tomorrow's news? This would have been immediately after the fact when a decision had been made that the Twenty-fifth Amendment wasn't going to be used. I said I would think about it and call back and talk again in the morning.

Overnight, after having been very reluctant in the beginning to suggest that a certain course of action should be taken, I changed my thinking. My first reaction was that this is a presidential prerogative, but the more I thought about it, I concluded: "This is damn well what we had in mind—this very kind of thing and somebody ought to say that."

QUESTION: Anesthesia is listed in your hearings?

SENATOR BAYH: This is exactly what we had in mind. The first section was "give it up, make sure that there is somebody there that can run the shop and then take it back again." Somebody needed to say that. In the meantime, something happened and Sam Donaldson or somebody got their attention and they decided to do something. The next time they shouldn't have to have that. If a blue-ribbon commission could make the next generation of presidents and presidential advisers aware of the fact that this is just business as usual and is nothing to spend a lot of time worrying about it, a president could make a plus out of it instead of botching it up. President Reagan could have gone down in history as the first person to have had the courage to use the Twenty-fifth Amendment. There are all sorts of things a blue-ribbon commission could do to help.

QUESTION: You say the educational effort or consciousness raising value of a commission might be its greatest contribution?

SENATOR BAYH: I would think that would be the least that could come out of it. It is certainly conceivable that something very positive in terms of supportive legislative enactments or revisions to the Amendment could also come. There is nothing sacrosanct about the Twenty-fifth Amendment. I can go down the list of shortcomings that you all have pointed out and say you are absolutely right; that's a problem there. But we were aware of most of them. I can also say if you solve that problem then you are going to have this new one and instead of having six peas on the scale you are going to put eight on the other side. It's a delicate balancing act in dealing with human nature.
　　The idea of pulling a president out of office kicking and screaming on television to go to some sanatorium is a horrendous thing to think about.

QUESTION: What about physical examinations?

SENATOR BAYH: Everybody feels they have to give an accounting of their health prior to the election. I wonder if there is any way of having that same requirement for the president, say once a year, like the rest of us. The president has a physical exam occasionally, but . . .

COMMENT: That is done not on a formal basis but on an *ad hoc* basis. Mr. Roosevelt had a physician and there are public reports about his various illnesses. The same thing happened with Eisenhower and Kennedy. I still think it comes back to the problem of the physician being very reluctant to say anything negative about his patient—the president. I understand that well. How could you ever have your patient trust you again? How would you get a patient to open up? How could he ever confide something embarrassing or something painful to a physician if he felt the physician might go public?

QUESTION: You mentioned the idea, I believe your phrase was, a "blue-ribbon commission" that might be put together to study this question and make a report. I was wondering if you had any precise ideas about the composition of such a body, be it in terms of the types of persons who ought to serve or of specific named individuals.

SENATOR BAYH: There are two types generally and I'm not sure which of the two takes precedent. I would recommend people that know the subject matter both from a constitutional and governmental aspect and from a medical aspect so that substantively it has credibility. I think probably equally important, considering the task, is to have at least some of those people chosen from organizations that have broad political support, public recognition and credibility so that whatever comes out of it would have a better chance of being accepted.

I know from my own personal experience that if we had just initiated this as members of Congress, we would have had a much more difficult time in getting general acceptance than was the case when we worked with the approval of the American Bar Association. I assume there are a number of medical groups similar to the Bar. As far as specific names, it would be nice if you could get one, or more than one individual who had actually been in the inner circles of White House deliberations.

QUESTION: Did you have a physician in the hearings? We can't find a physician either in the Kefauver hearings or in your hearings. Were there off-the-record consultations with physicians?

SENATOR BAYH: Yes, but not extensively so. We might have been in error there. Perhaps that was a shortcoming. We were willing to accept the worst case situation from a medical standpoint. It was not necessary for anyone to be persuaded that there were significant medical nuances and problems and that the severity of the various illnesses that could be dramatic as well as subtle. We looked at our mission as more of a political one as how to design and create a structure that would permit a system to go forward and take advantage of medical expertise at the time it would be needed.

I guess I have been, and we all have been, critical of past experiences, especially the way in which the Reagan team recently dealt with this. At the same time, I think we have to accept the fact that whatever action was or wasn't taken, the actors at the time believed they were doing what was right. I don't attribute any devious motives to the people who were acting. You mentioned Wilson's doctor; maybe he genuinely did feel that it would have killed Wilson to step down. I would assume that Meese and Baker and the people around President Reagan at the time of the assassination attempt didn't have much time to think about it. They were more concerned about whether or not he was going to live and what to do immediately—without figuring out what the Twenty-fifth Amendment required them to do.

QUESTION: I would like to ask, is it the duty of the physician to think solely of his patient and the patient's present and future well-being or is it also the duty of the physician to think of the nation?

DR. CRISPELL: That is very clear. In 1980, the American Medical Association (AMA) Council on Ethics revised the rules saying by law you've got to report venereal disease and non-self-inflicted gunshot wounds. That is the law for any patient. It doesn't matter who it is. It said specifically that if the physician feels that it is in the best interest of the country, he can break confidentiality.

DR. KNORR: That's why they're suing John Hinkley's former psychiatrist for not disclosing information that could have been relevant. Whether it would have done any good or not is another matter. Psychiatrists are now faced with this problem of confidentiality versus reporting someone who could be a real danger to the community.

QUESTION: Let's go back to this business that you brought up, Birch, about the physician before politicians are elected. I'm sure everybody knows that Roosevelt's physician told him that in no way should he run; he had a fatal illness. It hadn't been quite as fatal as everybody thought, but he went ahead and ran again. On the other hand, Morris Udall, after four neurologists convinced him not to run for president because he had Parkinson's disease is obviously still in the House. So you've still got this problem. If the doctor says you are unfit, the person can still go right ahead and do exactly what he wants, unless the doctor wants to blow it open to the public. So there is no protection from that standpoint and I can assure you, just from personal experience here in Virginia, that people are coming here and on two occasions wanted our physicians to make public announcements that they were in fine shape.

I think it is coming to the fore, but there is still this problem of the people around the president. The people who will lose the most if the president is declared disabled are the White House staff. They are protecting their livelihood in one sense, aren't they?

QUESTION: How did the Eagleton situation surface?

COMMENT: It was blown—one of the people that blew it won the Pulitzer prize. They probably got the information from a secretary at the Mayo Clinic. But they held it up. I happened to know the editor at the time. They held it up five days and consulted with McGovern before they blew the story to give Eagleton the opportunity to resign. The first day after the story started to surface, McGovern said he was in fine shape. Three days later, when the pressure really got on him via the *Detroit Free Press*, he asked Eagleton to resign.

QUESTION: To come back to the earlier question of the blue-ribbon commission, what was your attitude toward another cleavage in this sphere? Political scientists, who by and large aren't particularly known for embracing findings from other disciplines, are skeptical about how much you can say about the impact of health. Several political scientists were interviewed and they said an illness doesn't matter if the White House staff is in place. They said that Roosevelt, even with all his disabilities, was still better than some person who doesn't know the difference between Budapest and Bucharest. You get a cleavage on what the role of the physician ought to be. The political scientist certainly ought to have a role on the blue-ribbon commission, but what weight should he have? Did you, in not pushing hard for medical expertise, assume that there were political judgments in this area that transcended a lot of detailed medical information or didn't you talk much about that?

SENATOR BAYH: We talked about it. Here again, we thought the question was not so much determining whether the president was ill or not, but what to do if we had reason to believe he was. Having had that reason, then certainly we didn't want the chief of staff at the White House or the chairman of the Senate Judiciary Committee making that determination. You bring in your expert staff. The magic of the numbered days was arrived at by compromising the House and the Senate position. Between the two poles, the House position as I recall it was that it was too much time and that quick action was needed and that you couldn't afford to have somebody acting as president whose competence was under question. They felt it needed to be resolved quickly. The Senate wanted a little more time because it was such a critical decision that they felt they ought to make sure there was ample time to get all the evidence and to have hearings and have everybody operate on the basis of good, sound fact, not supposition. I don't think there is any magic time requirement. You can find out a lot of information in twenty-one days or two weeks for that matter.

QUESTION: Did the Brownell *Yale Law Review* article and the testimony he gave before the Kefauver Committee influence you when Brownell said doctors couldn't understand anything about politics?

SENATOR BAYH: I think so. You get back to the question of individual involvement of that personal doctor. It is awfully hard to envision a personal physician to someone like the president of the United States, who has been with him any length of time who is not going to feel very close to him and be protective of him. You get back to your standard view of ethics here. As I recall, what you just said was a permissive option and not a mandatory rule.

COMMENT: Not mandatory. Absolutely permissive like letting a patient die; it is the same sort of thing.

SENATOR BAYH: It may clear him of being sued for unethical conduct, but it certainly doesn't keep him hired as the president's physician. I don't know how words would protect against normal human relationships.

QUESTION: But you wouldn't rule out the medical component in all of this? If there was a group that was functioning in this blue-ribbon capacity, doctors ought to be there?

SENATOR BAYH: I certainly think so. They can deal very specifically with some of the nuances, for example, Alzheimer's disease and other illnesses that we know a lot more about now than we did earlier. They would probably make a much better case than a lay person could make about the impaired judgment that certain kinds of ailments bring. Besides, we are talking about presidential health from a credibility standpoint. You want somebody who knows something about health.

I guess the bottom line is how to convince a White House staff person that it is in his interest and in his boss's interest to do something that might potentially limit his power. None of us really wants to go to the bottom line if the trap door is going to be pulled from under you. I think probably most White House staff people do believe that it is very important for their president to be in control of things. These people feel very strongly that their president is very important to the health of the country and the safety of the world, etc, and they support him.

QUESTION: What are the long-term consequences of the president invoking Section 3? What if he says I require surgery for a polyp and I'm passing the power of the office on to the vice president? Is he going to pay politically for that as you see it? What are the consequences? How does it affect his possibility of reelection? Would someone say he's been disabled and is unable to serve again?

SENATOR BAYH: To me the argument is strongly in favor of going ahead and doing it. If you have him sneak off on some other pretense, the public is eventually going to know about it. I think it all depends on the manner in which you and your staff and your people handle it. This is a business as usual kind of thing and you can include some rhetoric about how this is going to be of a short-term duration. But the president is concerned about the country and wants to make certain that his good vice president who works closely with him can do whatever is necessary for the national interest which the president is unable to do. If it is a serious illness, being careful and prudent and following the Twenty-fifth Amendment doesn't make it more serious. If it is a minor illness, I don't think it makes it more serious either.

QUESTION: Does it make it more serious if you are the first to do it thus allowing somebody to say this must be of unprecedented historical gravity because it's the first time the Amendment has been invoked?

SENATOR BAYH: I suppose there is a possibility of that. But I believe that it makes it appear more as if you were trying to hide something by not using it than if you simply used it. Since Reagan has done it, regardless of what he calls it, everybody accepts the fact that the next president ought to be in the position of doing it without any fear or reservation.

It is never good to have to do something like this. Let's face it. Obviously, you'd like to have a president who could run the New York marathon every couple or three months, but presidents are human and some of them are going to get sick. And to the extent they get sick, the presence or absence of this provision will not cure them, but I think it makes the country a little less ill and a little more healthy.

QUESTION: Senator, earlier you reminded us that the veto would apply in the event of the exercise of this procedure. I assume it would also apply to the control of the "football." To what extent, if any, did you discuss possible philosophical differences between the president and the vice president—prior philosophical issues and differences about pending issues that might affect utilization during the transition?

SENATOR BAYH: We discussed that extensively. That is something that could well make a president more reluctant to use this amendment.

COMMENT: At least to delay it.

SENATOR BAYH: Yes, depending upon what the issue is. Let's take a dramatic difference in the philosophy of the president and the vice president. Most vice presidents would like to be president someday. The worst thing a vice president could possibly do politically would be to try to take advantage of the power that was given him by a temporarily ill president to promote his own ideas. So just from the standpoint of self-preservation, historically, vice presidents have always been reluctant to act. Then again, it all depends on how serious the illness is. If it is a temporary kind of thing, a matter of hours or a few days, unless the question is whether he should push the button or not push the button, then the vice president is not going to do that much damage in that time frame. Then again it would be self-destructive if he took advantage of that period which was supposed to be a ministerial period to turn it into a policy period. On the other hand, if the president is out of it and the vice president gains it involuntarily, then it is more difficult for the president to get it back. What we tried to create was an environment in which the president, given an illness, would be aware that the incentive was to do it voluntarily. This would decrease the reluctance to act voluntarily because the president would know that he could regain the powers without having to confront the vice president, the cabinet or the country.

NARRATOR: Could we talk for just a minute about any ideas anyone might have about possible changes, modifications, or statutory additions to the Twenty-fifth Amendment? We've had some proposals come up. It would be useful to have your reaction as to whether this kind of thing is worth looking into. One area was the role of the presidential physician. Dr. Ruge said if something was not right with the president's health he would feel perfectly free and indeed obligated to go to the attorney general or whoever was the proper person and tell him the president couldn't function. And he said he thought the physician—and the whole group of physicians sitting in the room agreed with him—was in a better, more detached and well-grounded position to do it than was the vice president. They kept saying the vice president was a party at interest. That group, if they had had to vote, would have voted just about unanimously in favor of reducing the power of the vice president and increasing the power of the presidential physician in this area. Is that worth talking about or is it so politically unrealistic given the processes of government so that one ought not even think about it?

SENATOR BAYH: I certainly think it's worth thinking about. When you have a room full of physicians sitting around being asked questions, I don't know how many of them are going to 'fess up. Many might have the attitude that I've gone fishing with this fellow for twenty years and I'm not going to pull the rug out from under him.

Maybe Dr. Ruge's relationship with President Reagan was different than past physicians. I would like to believe that a physician could make that detached determination.

35

I'm confident they could, but whether they would or not is the question. I guess if you took a room full of politicians they would opt for letting a politician make that decision and if you took a room full of doctors they would probably opt for a doctor. The doctor obviously has far more expertise than anybody else. But the politicians are the ones who must act.

QUESTION: What about a panel of physicians?

SENATOR BAYH: If the president's physician could get some help and if there were some procedure whereby he could get outside review or evaluation and if he could bring in physicians who were capable and could make judgments regarding the health, both physical and mental, of the president, then that would seem to me to be a reasonable kind of approach. I don't think the president's physician should make those judgments himself. I think if there were a process whereby he could initiate a medical inquiry into the health of the president and his ability to serve, I think that would be a good approach to it.

QUESTION: Should the physician's advice and counsel be mandatory or voluntary?

SENATOR BAYH: What about my concern about the permissive element of it? If you, in addition to setting up the review board or procedure where questions could be presented to a board for thorough study and made it a felony for the president's physician not to do so, that would maximize the chance of it being done and minimize the feeling that the doctor was going to be constantly looked down upon because he violated that patient/physician trust.

COMMENT: I think you could probably set up a board to help, but until you made this suggestion, I couldn't figure out how to make it legal. You could pick presidents of prestigious medical organizations who, from the day the president and the president's physician come into office, would be required to be on a consulting board. They would rotate every year if you picked medical association presidents. One of the points made by a U.Va. graduate who took care of a supreme court justice is that you get so involved in the confidentiality of the doctor/patient relationship that you lie to protect your patient. That is what McIntyre and Grayson did, of course. McIntyre blatantly lied about Roosevelt's health. But if you had an outside committee to give the president's physician support and they somehow become part of the recognized legal process, then it seems to me you would have a feasible system. I agree that you couldn't have one person deciding that the president is psychotic.

SENATOR BAYH: Aren't there various diseases nowadays that inflict us as human beings in which the character, background, stamina and response mechanism of the patient has a direct relationship to how severe the given problem is? What we are really after is such facts, not just a quick judgment. You can argue that maybe Roosevelt sitting there in the wheel chair was in better shape than somebody else or Eisenhower in an oxygen tent was better than somebody else. If it is just a panel of experts that look at that patient in a short time-frame, are they getting as good an assessment of how serious the effect is on the ability of that person to perform as is someone who has had a longer relationship? I'm not sure I know the answer to that question.

COMMENT: I think a diagnosis that describes a physical disorder in no way suggests the level of disability. If you have heart disease or the problem Roosevelt had, his mental acuity could have been just as sharp or sharper than someone who is one hundred percent able. It is the mental condition of the physical problem that really makes a person disabled or incapable of serving, I think. So, if you have a heart attack and you have serious heart disease, you are not incapable of serving, but if your heart disease has so depressed you that your mental state is slowed and you are incapable of making decisions, then you may be incapable of serving. Of course, in this instance you would hope that the president would say, "I've had a heart attack, I'm not up to it. Let's invoke Section 3; I need a break." You would hope everyone would agree and he would be applauded for so doing. If the disorder is a serious mental disorder, then the patient is usually the last one who has real judgment regarding his ability or disability. In fact, we see patients with mental disorders who feel they have unusual abilities and sometimes they are quite artistic and very impressive.

In that case you have a problem. It would take quite a bit of evaluation to judge them incapable. Being a psychiatrist and knowing what it is to go to court and try to get someone declared incompetent, I'll tell you you've got quite a problem on your hands. This is particularly true if it's the Captain Queeg type of illness where you know the man's judgment is impaired because of some mental disorder, but he is able to sit and be very reasonable and rational during a discussion.

QUESTION: Would there be a high political cost to a president who was subjected to this kind of a systematic evaluation and then found still capable of functioning? Would it seriously change the way that the president could continue to function with people that worked for him, with people in Congress and particularly with the public?

SENATOR BAYH: Yes, I think that is a very definite possibility. We don't want any trouble like that unless it is necessary. On the other hand, to argue my case for using the Twenty-fifth Amendment, if everybody has to do it then there is no down-side if it is done every year. But I can't imagine that particular scenario being accepted. If you could increase the responsibility of the president's physician so that he had no alternative but to do A, B, C, and D, if X, Y, and Z occurred, then you really put an increased responsibility on the one person that knows more than anyone else what to do with that information.

COMMENT: They do it in the armed forces—legally. An able medical officer at sea can take charge of the ship; he can relieve the captain. In SAC the physician can relieve any commander at any time.

SENATOR BAYH: A president's physician is a government employee, isn't he? He is paid by the government—not directly by the president. So the personal physician side of this is a little more cloudy.

COMMENT: Dr. Ruge is the first presidential physician in modern times to be non-military.

QUESTION: One of the reasons I think one feels it is so hard to be sure the physician is going to say something is the tendency to interpret the situation from your own perspective. What would it take for you doctors to go to Bob O'Neil [U.Va. President] and say that Mr. X or someone else has such and such a physical ailment and that as a physician you simply don't think that in their respective spheres they can do the job? Normally wouldn't the process be that a member of that person's board or a colleague would see some things and they would report them to President O'Neil? How do you do this in other spheres? How far do you think you should go?

COMMENT: I've done it twice—the University was suffering. They were not my patients and their doctors did not report. So I did.

COMMENT: I think probably Dan Ruge would have been secure enough to do this. He was sixty-four years old; he wasn't fighting for anything; he did not have a private practice; he wasn't worrying about being promoted to admiral. One of the problems with the military doctors is that they are worried about getting promoted if they do the right thing. Dr. Lukash was a captain and he moved up to the next rank. It would take somebody with great security, either financial or emotional, to do it. If Dr. Ruge reported that the President shouldn't do this or that, it wouldn't have hurt his career in any way. I think he would have been outspoken if needed. I think he has that kind of personality. But, I think a fifty year old person on the way up or trying to establish himself or worried about his career would have a hell of a time doing it.

SENATOR BAYH: Let's look at the alternative. Nobody likes to be in a position in which you are faced with jeopardizing your promotion because you have to squeal on the president. However, if indeed you don't and the law requires that you do, then five years later you find out you are subject to court martial and lose not only your promotion but your retirement.

COMMENT: I am very intrigued with your idea and would like to think further about how we could get the president's physician to be responsible to society.

SENATOR BAYH: In today's environment there would be those who would say this was just an effort to get a particular president. You get around that by making this effective four years from now. If you had a president's physician who said he would support this kind of thing, it would really help. This, of course, could be done by statute. There are weaknesses in the Twenty-fifth Amendment, but unless you can find something that makes it a lot better without at the same time making it a lot worse, I would urge you not to proceed along the constitutional amendment track. It is a nearly impossible track. We were just lucky to have had that little niche in time converge with the right players that got it done.

You could mandate that the president and vice president have a written agenda for what to do under given circumstances. Let two parties judge what should be done after deciding which problems the president wanted them to resolve or be prepared to resolve. Then require that to be passed on to each administration. In this crazy world we are living in, you could lose both the president and vice president at the same time. Hopefully that will never happen; I pray to God. But bringing in the legislative branch as a party would tend to lessen the political tension. And bringing the legislative and executive branches together could all be done by statute.

COMMENT: Cabinet members require congressional and senatorial approval. The president's doctor does not. Yet we've been talking about a power for the president's doctor which far surpasses that of any cabinet member.

SENATOR BAYH: Well, as doctors, you tell me: should my right to choose one of you as my physician be contingent upon you being able to satisfy a majority of the United States Senate?

COMMENT: One of the things which we asked Dan Ruge to do as a starter for us is to outline the duties of the president's physician. He called Bill Lukash, who was Ford's and Carter's physician, and they had a couple of hours together. The only time Lukash had any problem was when President Carter was going under surgery for his hemorrhoids. They had the Twenty-fifth Amendment ready, but other than that there was no occasion to worry about the Twenty-fifth Amendment. I must say I was pleased to know that Dan Ruge had really studied the Twenty-fifth Amendment and knew all about it. But, he wasn't asked anything about it during the shooting.

COMMENT: He carried it with him at all times. He took it very seriously. He was quite unhappy, I thought, with his lack of influence on the President and his treatment by the President's staff.

COMMENT: He said, for instance, that he thought Reagan traveled too much. He said he had lost all of his battles with the White House on that.

SENATOR BAYH: The other disconcerting thing was that Vice President Bush didn't know who he was. Bush met him in the hall one day and called him Max because he looked like somebody else on the White House staff.

QUESTION: Is the president's physician selected by the president?

COMMENT: Absolutely.

COMMENT: Nancy Reagan's stepfather, in effect, selected this one.

COMMENT: Dan Ruge was trained by Dr. Royal Davis; that's why he was there.

COMMENT: Dan Ruge had about ten consultants in to see the President during the first four years and I don't think anybody knew that or should they.

COMMENT: He said as a non-specialist he was more likely to bring people in.

COMMENT: He brought in Walter Guy who is now the President's physician; he brought his allergist back; he brought his neurologist back. None of this got in the papers. If the president's physician not only wanted to, but was in some way required to do this if needed, it could probably be done. But there is another problem that Dan Ruge didn't have. Some presidents have ducked their physician.

Everybody thinks that Janet Travell was Kennedy's physician. She wasn't the doctor physically present in the White House. There was another person who was the President's physician, but you can be sure that if Mr. Kennedy had anything wrong he either had Travell come down from New York, or he had a reason to go to New York. The reason Ruge could see the President whenever he wanted was the personal connection and because he could stand outside of his office and see the President coming from his bedroom to the White House offices. All I'm saying is that it would be possible for the president, if he really wanted to, to never see his physician.

NARRATOR: Thank you very much Senator Bayh for coming to the Miller Center and sharing your expertise and insights.

PRESIDENTIAL DISABILITY

Kenneth R. Crispell, M.D.

NARRATOR: Dr. Crispell's forthcoming book is about hidden illness in the White House. It seems appropriate to give you some biographical information about Dr. Crispell before he makes his presentation. He is a distinguished medical educator, university official, author, and member of many important scientific organizations and groups. He was born in Ithaca, New York, and educated in the Philadelphia College of Pharmacy. He did his post-graduate work at Cornell and received his medical degree at the University of Michigan. He interned in Robert Packer Hospital in Sayre, Pennsylvania, and did his residency in New Orleans at the Ochsner Clinic. He was a fellow in biophysics at Tulane.

He came as an instructor to the University of Virginia but not long thereafter became professor of medicine. Later he rose to become dean of the Medical School and then vice president for health affairs. He has been the moving force behind the Miller Center's interest in presidential illness, succession and the Twenty-fifth Amendment. We thought it most appropriate and long overdue that he speak about the question of presidential disability and the Twenty-fifth Amendment. It's a personal privilege for those of us who have worked with him to have Dr. Crispell with us.

DR. CRISPELL: Thank you. You might yourself ask why a pill-peddling doctor is talking about the presidency. Well, I've always been a history buff but did other things to make a living. My interest started through a series of circumstances which perhaps I should not discuss. I was invited to Haiti to see a very important person and I did not know who it was when I left New York. It turned out to be "Papa Doc" (the President of Haiti) and although he

43

had very bad press, I can tell you he was a delightful patient. My first experience with the press and confidentiality occurred then. The State Department said they would like to keep it quiet and I certainly wanted to keep it quiet, but as I got on the plane to come back the steward came up to me and said, "How's Doc?" I got home at about three o'clock in the morning and the phone rang at four o'clock. There was a woman reporter on the line who asked, "Doctor, how is President Duvalier?" And I said, "I don't know what you're talking about." She said, "Yes you do; we know when you got back and we'd like to have the story." I said that I had told the State Department that I would not give a story. She said, "Doctor, let me tell you what I'm going to print tomorrow morning in *Time*. I'm going to say you denied that you've been to Haiti."

I forgot all about it and I came back to Charlottesville. There one of our students who was a house officer at New York Hospital broke confidentiality and told me all about President Kennedy. He had been the house officer when Kennedy was admitted for his back surgery. So when I stopped shuffling papers, I thought maybe it would be fun to go back and look at history again from the standpoint of what happened when our leaders were ill. Did it change history?

I will begin my presentation with Wilson's presidency. Many of you are familiar with his history but I want to review it with you. I will also refer a good deal to Roosevelt because we have some new information through using the Freedom of Information Act. (Using the Freedom of Information Act took about two years. They are wonderful about sending hundreds of copies which mean nothing.) Then I'm going to spend some time on Kennedy and finally I'm going to deal with that part of the Twenty-fifth Amendment that I think has been most important for our current President. I'm going to leave the legality and all the problems of the Twenty-fifth Amendment to Paul Stephan. He and Dan Meador are really the experts on the Amendment.

Now as we go through this I want you to think about certain things. Does the public have a right to know if an elected official or candidate has an illness which will affect his performance? If the public knows, how does that affect the president and his physician in terms of the doctor-patient relationship? Think with me whether the illness of a public official has played a role in the decision making which has had major effects on national and international history. Then consider that again as we get to our current President. All the way through I'll talk about the coverup by presidential physicians, the White House staff's power to make decisions and then about the effects of a major illness on judgment. (I'll use slides to illustrate certain points.)

Let's start with Woodrow Wilson. Here is a slide of Wilson at the age of 54 in 1910 when he was elected governor of New Jersey, just before he ran for the presidency. By this time in his life he had already had two strokes. We call them TIAs (transient ischemic-attacks), meaning there is not a clot but a spasm from which one can recover. His illness was so bad while he was president of Princeton that he changed from writing right-handed to left-handed. He then recovered during this period until he went to the White House.

Let me say a word more about strokes. You can lose power in your hand. Look at his hand. He's in the lower left corner with a gnarled hand over his cane. This is two years into the presidency. I'm sure a lot of us have little strokes but Wilson's were major ones. One can recover from them especially with modern therapy but there was not therapy then. We know that he had severe high blood pressure at that time although the records of his physician have been destroyed. The records of his eye doctor who saw him in Philadelphia (a very famous man named De Schweinitz) indicate this. (You could tell high blood pressure by looking at the retina of the eye.) De Schweinitz at that time not only made a diagnosis of his high blood pressure but noted that he had had a clot in the carotid artery which had caused the stroke. Here he is on the way to the 1921 inaugural. The real president (Mrs. Wilson) is sitting on his left. She ran the government for eighteen months along with a very famous Senator from Virginia called Carter Glass. This slide is one of Wilson after the Paris Peace Conference. Historians may disagree but there are pretty good records that he was very sick in Paris. Actually one of our most famous graduates (Dr. Hugh

Young) went over to Paris to see him because he seemed to have a infected prostate gland. He was actually paranoid and he had a fever of 104 degrees. He thought that the maids in the palace where he stayed were spies. Then he came home and some eighteen bills came across his desk which he never signed. He lost the League of Nations and as you know he gave in to Lloyd George and Clemenceau during the Paris Peace Conference which could conceivably have been the cause of World War II because Germany was destroyed.

Now I will discuss some aspects of Mr. Roosevelt's presidency. In a photograph of the 1941 inaugural parade, Mr. Roosevelt looked quite happy. He was fifty-nine years old. The public didn't know that eleven years previously when he was governor of New York, his blood pressure was 200/110. Normal blood pressure ought to be something like 120/80. He already had had changes in his heart tracing. While governor he applied for an astronomical—at that time—life insurance policy of $500,000 and it took twenty companies to cover it. So they certainly knew there was something wrong with him at that time. The period when he was starting to feel the effects of his high blood pressure was probably 1941. We had no treatment for high blood pressure in 1941 except to go on a miserable low-salt diet. (I never had a patient comply with this diet.)

Now I show this slide because you can see Mr. Churchill in the lower right hand corner. This is December, 1941, after the attack on Pearl Harbor. At this time General Marshall and Churchill had the big battle over whether our army would attack through the Balkans or whether we should wait a year and go across the channel. The reason I show it to you is that Lord Moran, who was Churchill's physician, points out in his book that the night before (December 22, 1941), the British prime minister had had a severe heart attack. Perhaps this is why he gave up the next morning. I have had a heart attack and I would give up anything the next morning in the way of an argument. Whether this is the reason we went across the channel and not through the Balkans is for speculation.

Lord Moran has been in Charlottesville and when I was an arrogant young man I asked him why he allowed Churchill to take part in the conference. (He also didn't tell Churchill that anything had happened to him.) I said to Lord Moran, "I thought you had a responsibility to the country," but he looked me right in the eye and said, "I have a responsibility only to my patient."

I show this slide of a healthy-looking Harry Hopkins because I want to talk a little about the people around Roosevelt. I don't think there was a healthy person around Roosevelt. Louis Howe, with his asthma, was the sickest. Mrs. Roosevelt had built a special room in the White House for Mr. Howe and his incense that he used to burn for his asthma. Hopkins, soon after this, became seriously ill and went to the Mayo Clinic and had his stomach removed, ostensibly for cancer. In retrospect I have a friend who did the autopsy on Hopkins some ten years later who said Hopkins did not have cancer of the stomach. Rather he had a very unusual illness called Hemochromatosis which eventually did kill him.

Using that wonderful Freedom of Information Act, we found out that from around early 1943 until about March of 1944 Mr. Roosevelt was admitted to Bethesda twenty-eight times under assumed names: Joe Franklin, Joe Delano, etc. The only way we found out was by using the F. O. I. and a nice old naval captain whom we found. He was willing to tell us all the things that happened during that period. The correspondence between Steven Early and J. Edgar Hoover in the period just before the 1944 Normandy campaign reveals that there were leaks about FDR's illness. Mr. Early wrote to Mr. Hoover and said, "Someone is leaking information about the President's illness. I want it stopped." The leakage apparently came again when doctors broke confidentiality, probably by bragging, which usually ruins confidentiality. Apparently the radiologist at the Bethesda Naval Hospital had bragged at a cocktail party that he had just examined Mr. Roosevelt and that he had an enlarged heart. This started a whole series of questions.

By the time of the Yalta conference, FDR could sit up only about two hours a day. He was exceedingly short of breath and he already had what we in the medical profession call "chronic heart failure" and severe high blood pressure. Everybody was sick at Yalta. Churchill had suffered a coronary and probably had already gone through his first mild stroke (from which he had recovered.) Stalin

47

had had a coronary. He didn't fly and of course that is one reason the conference was at Yalta—because he could take a train there. Facetiously, the only healthy person in the famous picture of the Yalta conference was Alger Hiss.

The other point is that Harry Hopkins was the person who dealt with Stalin all during the war. They took him out of the Mayo Clinic on a stretcher and took him to Yalta because they thought his dealings with Uncle Joe were so important. My friends in history say it didn't make any difference whether Roosevelt was sick at Yalta or not: the cards were all stacked against him. As a physician I think it made a hell of a difference.

Next, I will cover some aspects of Mr. Kennedy's presidency. Before he arrived at the White House, he ran for Congress. At the end of the so-called "Bunker Hill Parade," which took place under very high temperatures, he collapsed and was taken to the home of one of his friends. As near as we can tell, he was given the last rites. He recovered from this and went on to win the election and go to Congress. Shortly after, when he arrived at the Congress in February 1948, he had a picture taken and he didn't look so healthy. His secretary made notes during 1948 and 1949 saying that he didn't do very much during that period except try to learn his way around Congress. The first evidence that we have that he was ill (other than what I've just talked to you about) came from a physician. Kennedy and Josh Billings went to Europe in 1946 and he left Josh in Germany and went back to London. From there he called his friend Pamela Churchill (who was no relation to Winston) whom he had met when he was over there with his ambassador father. Pamela called a doctor for him and the British doctor was shocked at his appearance and symptoms so they took him to a London clinic. The doctor telephoned Pamela and gave her his diagnosis. He said, "That young man friend of yours hasn't got a year to live." According to Pamela Churchill, Dr. David said that the patient had Addison's disease. He was lucky that he was born as late as he was because ten years previously he would have died in London because there was no therapy until about 1938.

The symptoms of Addison's disease—named after the very famous British physician who described it— include fatigue, weakness, craving for salt, fainting, lack of appetite, weight loss, and low blood pressure. The source of the problem is a deficient secretion of the adrenal cortical hormone. Kennedy's blood pressure in London was recorded at about 60/0—in that condition one doesn't live very long. The patient also has trouble with low blood sugar and salt retention. Then there is the symptom my friends who love Kennedy don't like: impaired judgment. I didn't say he had it, but that's a part of Addison's disease.

Then he went back to Boston. He apparently came home and saw Dr. Bartels, an endocrinologist. Dr. Bartels said he was not in crisis when he returned to Boston as he had been on active treatment. There are two types of treatment: one that keeps the patient alive and another that improves the patient's condition. He obviously had been on a synthetic material which was only enough to get him home. But as Bartels had noted he had had an episode of weakness, nausea, vomiting, and low blood pressure which had lead to the diagnosis.

A patient who dies from this disease goes through an Addisonian crisis. Fortunately I've not seen anybody experience one because therapy has been available since I've been in practice. After the diagnosis was made, JFK and his brother Robert went off to Okinawa and while there he had a very severe infection. His temperature went up to 106 degrees which is the beginning of an Addisonian crisis. Fortunately they got Dr. Bartels on the phone. He told them what antibiotics to use and Kennedy recovered but there is the question again of whether he didn't have the last rites in Okinawa.

All through the Pacific he had back pain. It's always been said that this was because he was on the coral reef for so many days. I'm not being nasty; I'm only trying to give you facts. He probably had a bad back when he went in. Perhaps the coral reef made it worse, but I was in the Army and there were an awful lot of people with bad backs who wanted to get out. He was discharged and went back to Boston and underwent surgery, but it was not really very successful.

When the presidential campaign started, Kennedy was in better health. He was now on adequate treatment but again there was a leak. First of all, however, you may remember that he came out with the boast that he was the healthiest candidate. That boast was against Johnson, of course, who had his coronary two years previously. Then the rumor emerged around Washington that he had an incurable illness. Here's what Pierre Salinger, Robert Kennedy, and JFK's physician, Janet Travell, put together. I'm going to quote it directly because this is the most amoral piece of journalism that I've ever read:

> John F. Kennedy does not now nor has he ever had an illness described as Addison's disease, which is a tuberculous destruction of the adrenal gland. Any statement to the contrary is malicious and false. In the postwar period he had some mild adrenal insufficiency. This is not in any way a dangerous condition. It is possible that even this might have corrected itself over the years.

This is an absolute lie. The reason I know is because I've seen hundreds of cases of Addison's disease. Yet I've only seen one case due to tuberculosis because we don't have tuberculosis any more. I can tell you that JFK did not have tuberculosis at autopsy. So this is fudging words.

They created this image of a young, heroic man, full of vital energy during the campaign and the media accepted it. I have asked C. R. Roberts, who was at the *Washington Post* at that time, why he didn't do anything about it. And his answer was, "Well the doctor said he was all right." Now that wouldn't happen today, would it?

At his inaugural he looked like a very happy man. Try to remember what he looked like when he was a congressman. Inauguration came after he had received adequate treatment for Addison's disease. The treatment has improved; I have a patient whom I treated twenty-one years ago and who writes to me occasionally indicating that she's fine. The only problem we have with Addison's disease is in the cortisone treatment. The problem involves the amount of cortisone that the patient should take. There is a wonderful feedback mechanism; if anybody is under stress the adrenal puts out more cortisone. If a patient is under stress, the question is whether he should take more cortisone or not. Well Kennedy did during the Cuban missile crisis. You'll see he has a very round face. He has swelling under the eyes and it is pretty obvious to a doctor that he had taken too much cortisone during this period in time. I wrote to my friend Lou Halle and told him that I was concerned about the fact that Kennedy had taken too much cortisone during the Cuban crisis. Lou in his usual fashion wrote back and said, "Well, if he did, I hope every leader in the country will take too much cortisone."

A common factor in all the examples I've used is the coverup element. Back to Wilson, Admiral Grayson told the public that the President was fine. They propped him up in bed, and let just a few visitors see him, which showed that he was fine. Those who remember Roosevelt's day may recall that McIntire said that FDR was just fine for his age, considering his polio. Even in his memoirs McIntire wrote that there was really nothing seriously wrong with him. There are also records of the physician who came down from Atlanta to see Mr. Roosevelt while he was at Warm Springs. There wasn't any question that this man was seriously ill. There were complete coverups by Admiral Grayson and by Admiral McIntire for Roosevelt, and even a more serious one by Janet Travell for Mr. Kennedy. Did these illnesses change the world? Vice President Marshall left Washington because he didn't want to take over for Wilson. When Truman took over for Mr. Roosevelt he had no information about what was going on in the world. (He was called the haberdasher from Kansas City.) One of the things we know (even though much of it remains classified) is that Truman only got Secret Service protection for the first time about three months before Mr. Roosevelt died. His first question to the Secret Service was, "What the hell are you doing here?"

Now I will briefly discuss the Twenty-fifth Amendment. We became intrigued with it when we did some research and found out that things were starting to happen way back in the Kefauver era when President Eisenhower was sick. Kefauver headed a committee to look into the possible outcome if Eisenhower couldn't continue to govern. The committee started its work, but then Kefauver died during the hearings and nothing was done until after JFK was killed. At that time Senator Birch Bayh, who was a young senator from Indiana, apparently had nothing else to do (so he says), so he pushed this amendment. He and Mr. Herbert Brownell, who helped work out the Eisenhower agreements, were probably most responsible for the amendment.

The Amendment was enacted in 1967 and in most cases it superceded the Presidential Succession Act which I'll mention briefly. In the two new issues that I'm going to discuss, it provides for both voluntary and involuntary removal of a president from office—which we've never had—and the presidential appointment of a new vice president. This has happened twice: first, when Nixon appointed Ford and then when Ford appointed Rockefeller. There is a part of the Amendment that is relevant for President Reagan. It says that:

> He voluntarily transmits his inability to serve. He must do this in writing to the speaker of the House and President Pro Tem of the Senate. The vice president becomes the acting president with all rights and privilege belonging to the office. The acting president continues in this capacity until such times as the president transmits in writing to Congress his or her ability to serve again.

The next article is the tough one, involving a process which the Presidential Disability Commission is examining. This article would apply if the president were crazy, or if he were involuntary deemed unable to serve. Action must be initiated by the vice president and a majority of the Cabinet or another body provided by law such as Congress. In most cases action will involve the vice president and the majority of the Cabinet.

After the vice president sends a letter, Congress must assemble within forty-eight hours to debate the issue. Congress has twenty-one days to decide whether a president is unable to serve. Should they decide a president is unable to serve they must do so by a two-thirds majority of both Houses, otherwise the president continues in office. This number is higher than impeachment, which requires a 51 percent majority.

What are some of the problems and ambiguities? If the president is unable to serve for whatever reason, how many times may he or she appeal the decision? Some may think it's clear from a legal standpoint, but as a novice, I wonder if a president couldn't keep on insisting that he is fit for office.

This is the problem we've studied during five sessions of the Miller Center Commission: what constitutes the inability to serve or discharge the duties of the president? Is it merely medical or does it cover political inability? I personally don't know the answer. After I talked to Senator Bayh, I think the authors of the amendment were referring to medical disability though no physicians appeared before the congressional committee. Nonetheless, there is some possibility for a *coup* to develop. The vice president and the House could say, "Let's get rid of this guy; we don't believe in him anymore," and then take him to Congress. However this scenario is probably very far-fetched under the American system. A presidential unwillingness to make decisions also worries me a little bit. Mr. Bayh has told us that they wanted continuity; they wanted the government to keep on running. That is the main theme of the whole constitutional amendment.

Now we come to perhaps the toughest problem. What is the responsibility of the examining physician if he uncovers a serious illness which the patient (who happens to be our president) wishes to keep confidential? We run into the whole business of doctor-patient confidentiality. The council on ethics of the AMA says that one can break up a doctor-patient relationship if it's for the benefit of the community. In that case I worry about the people in my profession. Are they competent to judge the extent of an illness or the mental stability of a patient, especially when it comes to judgment? There is also the aspect I mentioned previously: it takes twenty-one days to get to a decision. What effect would this crisis have on foreign policy, on activities of the military, etc.? There's another worry: the nuclear code. It has to go with the president wherever he goes. Three members of the Secret Service are responsible for the code, one of whom has "the football." It used to be called the "red button" but I understand now the parlance in Washington is "football."

I'll briefly discuss the assassination attempt upon Reagan, which is related to our subject. Vice President

Bush, who was on his way to Houston, was asked to turn around and come back. Edwin Meese and James Baker were probably over at George Washington Hospital. Fred Fielding, who was legal counsel to the President, had already prepared the papers for section 3 or section 4 of the Twenty-fifth Amendment. This took place during a crisis situation. The President was in semi-shock, about to undergo surgery.

Richard Darman who was in charge of all the papers the President was supposed to sign (conscious or unconscious, I guess) took them and placed them in a safe. So for a period while he was under surgery, as far as I'm concerned, we didn't have a president. Al Haig came up with his famous "I'm in charge" statement. Why did he think he was in charge if he was fifth in line?

One of the intriguing questions is who had the nuclear code during this period while Reagan was under anesthesia. So far we haven't been able to find out and probably will never be able to find out. Several members of the committee, including Kenneth Thompson and myself, have had the opportunity to visit with Dr. Dan Ruge who was the presidential physician during the shooting and with Dr. Bill Lukash who had that same position for three presidents. Dan Ruge took the President to George Washington Hospital and he then turned him over to the people at the hospital. Afterwards he was never consulted again by any member of the White House staff as to whether the President should invoke section 3 or section 4. The morning after the shooting (after the President waved and said he was fine) Baker called Ruge and asked him to talk to the White House staff and then Bush called him in to talk to the members of the Cabinet. The only question asked of Dr. Ruge was whether the President was all right, and his answer was affirmative as far as he knew. My point is the White House staff made all the decisions during that period of time without any information from the physician.

This is what happened during the cancer surgery when the President had ten days to prepare the world for the surgery. He did not invoke section 3. Instead he wrote this letter which in part says, "After consultation with my counsel and attorney general, I am mindful of the provisions of section 3 of the Twenty-fifth and of the uncertainties of

54

its application to such brief and temporary periods of incapacity." If you look at the hearings during the Twenty-fifth Amendment debate, however, anesthesia was one of the things mentioned as a proper reason to invoke section 3. He said: "I do not believe the drafters of this amendment intended it's application to situations such as this." You make up your own mind.

Now the final question is whether he made some mistakes following cancer surgery. The *Los Angeles Times* recently reported that "despite earlier White House denials, President Reagan may have approved the first shipment of U.S. arms to Iran while ill or under sedation [this is after surgery], a condition that may have left him unable to recall his actions." Later Attorney General Meese told the House Intelligence Committee, "The explanation is that Reagan was either in the hospital or recovering." Representative Brown gave the impression that it was a difficult time for the President. It certainly would have been for anybody. That explanation lends additional credence to the former national security adviser McFarlane's contention that he received oral approval from Reagan for the deal. Reagan underwent surgery on July 13. The first arms shipment occurred the next month. Brown quoted Meese who testified behind closed doors saying that the meeting between McFarlane and Reagan would have been private.

In 1964 during the hearings for the Twenty-fifth Amendment, Truman said, "I don't think in the enormous emergency that we would be faced with under circumstances if the president did become disabled, that we could wait much longer in meeting the problem. We must face it and solve it or else we could find ourselves in an extremely grave situation if we continue to leave it to chance." I think it still true in 1987 although some of my colleagues may disagree. And Dean Rusk said this right after he left office: "The international list of those who carry great responsibility while ill is long and there are fleeting glimpses of the decisions which good health might have turned in other ways." I agree with this. My friends in history don't.

Finally, for a bit of levity, I have an aphorism: "I've learned to use bifocals, my dentures fit me fine, I could

55

live with my arthritis but I surely miss my mind." That was *not* by President Reagan.

QUESTION: There must be some times such as during Roosevelt's presidency during the war years when there has to be confidentiality between the president and his physician. How does that square with the Twenty-fifth Amendment?

DR. CRISPELL: Your first statement is correct. I think that if Truman had been taken into confidence, or had not believed McIntire perhaps, it would have been a lot easier for President Truman when he finally took over. He apparently really didn't know anything about the President's illness because FDR spent the last eight months at Warm Springs rather than in Washington. I don't know the answer to your question. I still worry about the case of war. Ken Thompson has taught me that the aides and the White House staff actually run the government. My problem is they make the wrong damn judgments medically.

COMMENT: When we began this project, if we had taken a vote among the political scientists here and elsewhere, we would have decided not to do it. But this isn't the first time we've tried something the conventional wisdom said we ought not to try. The argument political scientists make—seventy or eighty percent of them—is that the White House staff is closest to the president. They are most experienced in the work at hand and they see the president every day. They know whether he can make decisions or not make decisions and therefore you shouldn't worry too much. Another argument they make is that things continue to function when a president is in the hospital. You have a Jim Baker and he does take on the task.

One interesting thing that has happened in this commission is that people like Mr. Brownell have become much more open to and respectful of the judgment of the presidential physicians who have come before the commission. They ought to know something about the business of health and I think that has been useful. If this commission says anything new, I suspect it will be drawn out of what the doctors have said.

The executive vice president of the AMA made a long intervention at the last meeting arguing that there is an analogy with the AIDS epidemic so far as the national interest and the welfare of the nation is concerned. His argument was that we are now thinking in terms of thousands of cases. If this virus *does* become active among people who have been exposed, you could be talking in terms of millions by the 1990s. If that level is reached, then isn't it the duty of the physician to report the condition of a patient who may be a part of this chain of spreading infection? The analogy was that where the survival of the planet is involved, the presidential physician has the duty to go immediately to the vice president or to the president's wife if she is influential or anybody who is likely to influence the invoking of the Amendment and say that the president is unable to serve. I think the Commission found that part of the discussion quite instructive. Of course, there is also the concern that a physician who tries to invoke the Amendment could be fired.

QUESTION: One troublesome problem is that we're painting a picture of relative absolutes: the president is capable or incapable. From the perspective of our foreign policy, once the issue of the president's competence has been raised, his ability to negotiate deals is substantially hampered. I don't think that in medical terms there is such clarity as to whether the president is capable or incapable. To what extent can we legitimately wait before questioning presidential competence without jeopardizing the presidency in general?

DR. CRISPELL: It's a key question. When does the physician say he's crazy? One of the terrible things that we face in this country is Alzheimer's disease which is a classic example of the problem. First, let me make it perfectly clear that I don't think the President has Alzheimer's. Yet I think this is the type of illness that is going to be exceedingly difficult for a presidential physician or a group of physicians to identify and decide about a patient's mental capacity and ability and whether he can communicate. As Dr. Schwarz brought out in our discussion, the troubling thing is it will probably go far down the line before a physician will say the president can't function. I think it was an easy decision under Reagan's recent surgery; the whole world should have accepted anesthesia and major surgery as serious incapacity. Most people have had some kind of surgery and know how hellish they feel for forty-eight to seventy-two hours afterward. It was a big mistake not to use the Amendment during that period. The President's physician did not make that decision. The White House staff with inadequate medical information made the decision. Anesthesia followed by drugs followed by recovery are more than enough to incapacitate anyone. Sure he could wave out the window as he did eight hours after cancer surgery but for God's sakes it is foolish to try to run the government with a hole in your belly.

Getting back to the case where a president slowly loses judgment (and getting close to President Reagan's age I understand that), I think it will be exceedingly difficult for anybody to intervene. I would like to see something comparable to Mr. Brownell's arrangement in the 1950s. There was an agreement before the fact between Nixon and Eisenhower. At that time the country wasn't very worried about Ike though it probably should have been. Nixon was there and Brownell satisfied the nation. Yet it seems to me that one of the things that we could do before the president takes office is to have a meeting of the vice president, the legal counsel and the president's physician. They could get together and the physician could say, "I will find out when to come to you, Mr. Vice President." But the president might fire that guy on the spot.

QUESTION: What do other countries do about this?

DR. CRISPELL: I've written to all my friends in England and of course they don't worry about this. They could get rid of Margaret Thatcher in a hurry, because the party leadership is already in place to take over the reins of power. In short, other systems are better prepared for this than we are.

QUESTION: What worries me is the breach of confidentiality for the benefit of the community. That seems a very ambiguous thing to me. For example, a

Kenneth R. Crispell, M.D.

removal of Roosevelt would have put Wallace into the presidency. That might have indicated a different view of what is in the benefit of the community than if you put Truman or John Nance Garner into the presidency. Rumors associated with Kennedy's selection of Jacobson as his physician are very nasty.

DR. CRISPELL: Yes, he was the amphetamine peddler in New York. (Amphetamine is the upper.) He injected them, the worst method possible. According to his memoirs he treated Hollywood stars and other luminaries including Kennedy. Of course, we can't verify any of this. Thank God he's dead. Supposedly Kennedy was high at the Berlin Wall for instance and shortly after he stopped. I think we have to classify that as a rumor, though.

QUESTION: Nevertheless is it possible for a president to choose a physician who will go along with his own politics?

DR. CRISPELL: Oh, absolutely! Nancy chose Dr. Ruge. Dr. Ruge was her father's partner in neurosurgery. Dan happened to be a wonderful neurosurgeon and also a very good physician and anytime the President was ill, he brought a consultant in the side door. I don't know anything about the President's friend from Los Angeles that came in to follow Ruge. Now there is an army person. Having been in the post, Ruge and Lukash, who met with us, wondered if there should be a more official recognition of the president's physician.

QUESTION: Did they recommend a selection by someone other than the president?

DR. CRISPELL: Well, they didn't know how to do it. As somebody said, "It's a white collar job. It's only an item on the budget. Prior to the Twenty-fifth Amendment maybe it meant nothing at all." I personally don't know.
During the Twenty-fifth Amendment hearings in 1963 Truman suggested the creation of a committee of seven to decide, constituted of two members from the House, two from the Senate, two from Justice and one other person. They would decide about the president's ability, but they

59

would be in consultation with four medical leaders. I have some objections. First of all, it is almost impossible to get seven people to agree and four doctors to agree, so there is going to be a delay. I think the question is really one of judgment and it is difficult for anybody to decide about his judgment.

If this statement from the *Los Angeles Times* is correct, I think the White House staff made a terrible error after Reagan's surgery for cancer. If I'm not mistaken, the President said on television the other day after the Iran-contra hearings that he wondered if he made a decision while he was ill. Didn't he say that in his radio address? We've met with the legal counsel, Fred Fielding, who visited the President after cancer surgery, and he told us that he and Donald Regan made the decision for the President to resume the office. They made the decision. We asked Mr. Fielding about it and he said "Well the surgeon said he was ok." Well what a surgeon means by "ok" is that he survived the operation. They didn't question him about the President's judgment. It was a terrible thing for the President to be brought back to office. Again he could have waved from the room and I think people would say, "My goodness, isn't it wonderful that he's so well."

QUESTION: Some of the previous presidents who were critically ill were in their early fifties. Industry feels justified in making the head of a large corporation retire at 65 when his responsibilities must be minor compared to those of the president of the United States. Is there not some justification for putting an upper limit on the age at which a man can serve? We have a lower limit of thirty-five.

DR. CRISPELL: I suspect the answer depends on the age of whoever poses the question. I certainly don't think anybody should be on the Supreme Court or be President of the United States after 65. I have some of my marbles left but believe me, after that age it is very easy to get very tired unless you are a very unusual person. And the presidency is the worst job in the world unless one turns it over to subordinates as apparently Reagan has done. I doubt that either branch of Congress will touch the age business.

Certainly not until Claude Pepper, our distinguished congressman and former senator from Florida, leaves this world.

QUESTION: But can't the judiciary and the legislative branch afford a few people whose memories are not good? It's the executive branch that can't afford to have an individual who doesn't have the capacity to mobilize all his mental facilities.

DR. CRISPELL: Yes, in this case the damage of such people is diluted. Felix Frankfurter sat on the bench of the Supreme Court for nineteen months and they brought him in and propped him up. We have had Russell Long and all of our other friends on alcohol in the Congress but that's all diluted I think. When you get to the presidency, there's the heat in the kitchen. I think that's the problem.

QUESTION: I ask concerning the phrase "political inability." Most of us would think that the medical questions were really secondary to that. The political ability or inability seems to be the real subject of judgment. Looking back at the three cases as a historian, how would you apply that notion to those three men? Was "political inability" the determination of their incapacity?

DR. CRISPELL: Well as you know it's a big guesstimate. Consider Wilson with Lloyd George and Clemenceau in Paris. They were destroying Germany. Wouldn't it have been better to have Marshall who was Wilson's vice president?

I think in retrospect that Harry Truman was a pretty sharp fellow. And you know he had to do a tremendous amount of work before Potsdam because he had really no information. Of course he was dealing with Churchill's successor.

COMMENT: But people didn't think he was sharp.

DR. CRISPELL: No, it's history that says he was sharp. I can't answer the question. Do you think any member of the Kennedy family would have wanted Lyndon to become president? Let's go back to the basic part of your question.

What I've learned in dealing with these pros is that it always is necessary to consider political consequences. I feel almost on the end of the diving board with such pros because their question always comes back to something like your question: "Is it politically expedient to make this change?" (Despite the fact that you have to lock the president in his room so he can't get on the tube.)

NARRATOR: We're terribly grateful for Ken Crispell. Like many others he has been a prophet without honor, at least as far as the social sciences are concerned, because he's been lecturing and discussing this problem around the country, but not at the Miller Center. We thought it was high time he did it here. I think the most important aspect is that he has begun a conversation on whether or not we have arrived at answers on political or medical questions. There are people who have said that we should keep the doctors out. Every time we suggested a doctor on the Commission somebody would say, "Another one?" We had that debate, but I think anyone from the Miller Center Council would agree that this is what Mr. Miller thought we ought to be doing. We must discuss problems with people who have diverse points of view and bring the public together to hear the principal thinkers and leaders in the field. We intend to do so with Paul Stephan who will bring a legal insight to the problem which is different from the political insight of the people who faced this question when the Twenty-fifth Amendment was drawn up. I know we are all terribly grateful to Kenneth Crispell. Thank you.

HISTORY, BACKGROUND AND

OUTSTANDING PROBLEMS OF

THE TWENTY-FIFTH AMENDMENT

Paul B. Stephan III

NARRATOR: We've heard from the members of the medical profession on at least one occasion and now it's time to hear from the lawyers. I've observed that there are basically two views of lawyers: one is the view of lawyers as "suffering servants", the view that John Rockefeller III used to express. He would say, "If this lawyer doesn't tell us what we want to hear, get another lawyer." The other view presents lawyers as advocates of permanent written rules and statutes. It is striking on crucial issues how often reference to statutes, for instance, occupies the center of the discussion.

In a recent meeting of this Commission, there was an intriguing exchange between representatives of two points of view. One was advocated initially by former Attorney General Brownell who basically argued that the presidential physician would be in a stronger position if there were a statute providing that, where serious disability occurs, he would have every right to depart from the usual doctor-patient relationship of confidentiality. Advocates of the opposing view held that a statute wasn't necessary because it was already well understood that in matters of community interest the physician had an obligation to let the facts be known. Through this whole process, it has been enormously helpful to have Paul B. Stephan III, professor of law at the University of Virginia Law School participate in our discussions. He has contributed not only as a participant at the meetings but with great skill as a draftsman. This is another function where lawyers often perform best. They get the conclusions down in hard print that otherwise could be debated and contested for years to come. So it is appropriate and natural for Mr. Stephan to meet with us and present some of his thoughts. He has also researched the history of the Twenty-fifth Amendment about as thoroughly as anyone we've met in the course of these deliberations. It is a great pleasure to have him with us.

PROFESSOR STEPHAN: Thank you for that generous introduction. In terms of my involvement in this topic, there really is a strange confluence of factors here. I am generally interested in constitutional questions that deal with the separation of powers. For people of my generation, people who went to law school during the Watergate hearings, it's a natural attraction. It turns out that I have a particular, although indirect, tie to the Twenty-fifth Amendment because one of my first employers and someone I like to consider my mentor, Justice Powell, is one of the authors of the Twenty-fifth Amendment. This fact doesn't really come through too well in Birch Bayh's book. Bayh is certainly, along with Herb Brownell, one of the draftsmen, but there really were three important players in the original creation of the Twenty-fifth Amendment: Herb Brownell, who was the attorney general during the Eisenhower administration; Birch Bayh, who as a junior senator from Indiana saw a possible constitutional crisis in our lack of a vice president in 1963 after the Kennedy assassination; and Lewis Powell, the head of the ABA during this period. The three of them played a very important role in both the drafting of and in rallying popular support for the Twenty-fifth Amendment.

This also is a project that involves confluence of law and medicine, and I have both a general and particular interest in that. As I like to say, I sleep with a doctor. My wife is a physician and through the experience of putting her through medical school, I have acquired at least an interest if not an expertise in these problems. And I actually have a very particular interest in a different set of health problems of leaders. In my misspent youth before I went to law school I worked for the government in an agency that I do not care to identify at which we began the

"Brezhnev death watch" back in 1974, ending only eight years later. Of course, there were two new death watches immediately following. So I've actually studied in some depth before ever coming into this project the other nuclear power and the other trembling hand on the button, so to speak, and looked at the interplay of institutional factors and the personal health of the other leader. It was quite clear that Brezhnev from at least 1975 was infirm although not necessarily incompetent. For all these reasons, when Mr. Thompson asked me to take on this subject and serve as counsel to the commission, I cheerfully agreed.

In essence, I have done research on the background and history of this amendment, trying to identify both the explored and perhaps the unexplored legal problems that are generated and to look at the application of this legal text in a particular context. It was serendipitous that the most important applications of the amendment occurred after the work of the Commission actually began. We were well under way in the late spring of 1985 when President Reagan had his intestinal surgery. It was the first time that any president has ever actually invoked the Twenty-fifth Amendment, although Ken Crispell and I don't entirely agree on whether in fact he did. Then more recently this past January there was another health issue during which it is arguable that President Reagan should have invoked the Twenty-fifth Amendment, although he did not. So we have a more vivid context for this in the last few years and it is no longer simply an academic discussion. We have live issues involving this amendment.

Before getting to the context let me go back and refer to the amendment itself. It actually has packed into it a number of different tasks. They all deal with succession but in regard to quite different problems; the first three have historical precedents and the fourth section confronts a crisis that has not yet arisen, or at least not clearly. Section One settles an old debate over the status of the vice president when he succeeds to the presidency; in other words, the debate between whether he is simply an acting president or if he is the president in full. It was never completely clear to me what hung on that distinction but it did matter sufficiently to President Tyler that when he succeeded William Henry Harrison, he took the oath of presidential office rather than simply relying on the responsibilities that flow from his prior election as vice president. Section one confirms that result by saying that in case of removal, the vice president becomes president.

We all know Section Two from the Watergate crisis; it was invoked in rapid succession twice. The problem that motivated Birch Bayh after Kennedy's assassination was to define, once a vice president has taken over as president, who occupies the vice presidency. There is no successor designated in the Constitution as such. Succession has been provided for by Congress at different times and with different rules. For example, it may be a little known fact that Harry Truman's successor in 1945, under the succession statute then in effect, was the secretary of state who happened to be Republican. If anything had happened to Truman there would have been a change of parties in government. That was altered by the 1947 Act which made the speaker of the House and then the president pro tem of the Senate next in line of succession, thus short-circuiting the Cabinet succession.

Until the Twenty-fifth Amendment was promulgated, though, there was no provision for appointing a new vice president. As we all remember, of course, that was the provision that President Nixon relied on to replace Vice President Agnew with Vice President Ford. In turn Ford relied on it to appoint Vice President Rockefeller. It turned out to be a very useful provision. Try to imagine the dimensions of the Watergate crisis had Carl Albert been next in line if Nixon had been impeached; had Agnew simply gone to jail and there had been no new vice president, that would have been the situation. Bayh was most attentive to this problem and in that sense I think this provision of the Twenty-fifth Amendment worked very well.

Section Three of the Twenty-fifth Amendment deals with a sick president who knows he is sick and wishes to make a temporary provision for his incapacity. This was really Herb Brownell's experience. He observed two different health crises during President Eisenhower's administration. During the second one they were very attentive to these issues and as he has revealed in both public and private contacts and in the deliberations of our Commission, they ultimately made an *ad hoc* decision. Since there was not much cooking at the time and no international crisis in effect, there was no immediate need for a designated president. They addressed the situation but they did not implement any decisions as to what to do with Richard Nixon. They were fully prepared if anything arose to have Nixon serve as acting president during Eisenhower's crisis and then have him step back into the role of vice president once Eisenhower recovered his health. The occasion did not arise. Eisenhower was sick enough but there was no urgent matter that needed a presidential attention. It was a good stop-gap solution but there was no clear constitutional authority for doing this.

Consequently, the Twenty-fifth Amendment created a mechanism within the Constitution to authorize a procedure for a president to say in effect, "I am unable to serve temporarily. Rather than resign the office, I will temporarily remove myself and have the vice president serve as acting president." The difference is that an acting president can go back to the office of vice president, something a vice president who succeeds by death or resignation or impeachment cannot do. When the president feels he has recovered his powers, he again invokes Section Three of the Twenty-fifth Amendment to terminate the acting presidency of the vice president and then resumes office.

President Reagan appeared to invoke this provision. In fact I would say he *did* invoke it in July of 1985 during his surgery, though the text of the letter doing this is ambiguous. We will return to this topic, but with a caveat I would be prepared to say that President Reagan actually did invoke it. His lawyers certainly meant him to do that as they have told us in meetings with them.

That leaves the most tantalizing, and so far the only unused provision of the Twenty-fifth Amendment: Section Four. It deals with a crisis that our nation has never directly confronted although, arguably, we did go through it at the end of Wilson's presidency. Namely, it involves a sick president who refuses to accept the existence of his disability. Other than impeachment there had been no mechanism for dealing with an unfit president, and in the case of illness, impeachment doesn't seem like an appropriate mechanism because after all it is designed to deal with high crimes and misdemeanors. Illness just doesn't fit into that category. Impeachment is also irrevocable, and although Wilson was probably incurably ill, one can envision situations where a temporary illness affects the officeholder. Furthermore, there may be situations where the president is unable to invoke a temporary transfer of power because of the suddenness of the crisis. Perhaps the assassination attempt on President Reagan was such a case. Although he was conscious for some minutes, things were happening so quickly that the staff frankly had other things on their minds—like keeping him alive. So they did not really confront the issue of succession.

The Justice Department is worried about a hypothetical situation where the president is taken hostage. Arguably at that point, nobody would want that person to be our president, although once the emergency is over we certainly would want to restore his powers.

Section Four can apply to any of those situations. It involves situations where a president is unwilling to confront his disability, or where he is unable to do so because of the suddenness of health emergencies or other kinds of emergencies. In all situations the mechanism is not expeditious. Congress was very concerned about a mechanism that would remove the president even temporarily which could be used against the president's will. The model they had in mind was impeachment. Indeed just as a procedural matter, ultimately this mechanism is tougher to make stick, I would say, than impeachment.

Section Four operates in two stages. First of all, there has to be a decision to remove the president and make the vice president the acting president. This decision requires the consent of the vice president and of a majority of the Cabinet. The amendment has built into it the authority of Congress to create some other body to substitute for the Cabinet. There were many ideas circulating. Indeed Ike supported the idea of a blue ribbon commission as the entity that would temporarily remove a president. Authorities such as the head of the American Medical Association (AMA), the Chief Justice, the speaker pro tem or the speaker of the House, could be members of the commission. The framers of the Twenty-fifth Amendment did not want to go this route but they didn't want to preclude it either so they left this mechanism in Section Four. Congress, if it chooses to do so, can substitute for the Cabinet with a blue ribbon commission, but the vice president can't be replaced. He cannot become the acting president if the president objects unless he affirmatively consents to that step.

The president then can object. He would not in situations where he is simply unconscious or incommunicado, but he might when he is sick and does not realize it, as was arguably Wilson's situation. At that point Congress becomes the referee. During the period of conflict the vice president as acting president remains in this position. This is pretty clear both from the language of the amendment and from its history although some authors, in particular Ed Yoder, have written things that suggest the opposite. I would just say they are wrong. (That's one of the virtues of being law professor, you just point out the mistakes.) Congress, though, is the decision-making body. Congress must act within twenty-one days; if they do not then the president automatically resumes his powers. Each House of Congress must endorse by a two-thirds vote the vice president as acting president. This procedure is tougher than impeachment which requires only a majority of the House although it does require two-thirds vote of the Senate.

In a real conflict, many safeguards make it very hard to keep a sick president out of office for long. That was a deliberate decision; it may have been mistaken but Senator Bayh's account of these procedures reveals that there was a lot of concern. He points the finger more at Senator Robert Kennedy than at anyone else. Kennedy, as he describes it, pulled him aside and told him that very serious safeguards were required in order to obtain his support. That in essence is our legal structure. We have a mechanism that runs smoothly for sick presidents who want to take advantage of it. We have a mechanism, although not a very smooth or expeditious one, for sick presidents who do not want to take advantage of it. We do have a mechanism to cover the situation of an unconscious president, such as President Reagan's situation when he was on the operating table after the assassination attempt.

will examine briefly the context. First, I'll consider President Reagan's assassination attempt. In order for him to have invoked Section Three of the Twenty-fifth Amendment—the voluntary temporary transfer—a standard operating procedure would have been required to be in effect. That would allow the Secret Service to be ready to act. It's debatable whether such a procedure ought to be in existence. It may be argued that during a crisis situation it is not appropriate to make a decision as weighty as a transfer of power and all that goes with it. This point of view maintains that it cannot be a snap decision.

My point of view would be the opposite. If it is a standard procedure and it is clear that the president is going to lose consciousness soon, then there is no reason, as a matter of automatic procedure, not to sign the transfer of power so that the vice president can assume his responsibility. To be sure, it may have been unnecessary in the case of the assassination attempt to have a boss. There was no crisis then that demanded that we have an acting president. On the other hand, there was a kind of crisis in confusion over the line of succession. ·The journalists' accounts indicate that Al Haig said to Fred Fielding "You'd better go back and read your Constitution, buddy." I'm not sure we should rely on these accounts, but if they are true Haig got the succession flat wrong. The answer is not in the Constitution, but in the Succession Act in a case where the vice president is out of the picture as he was then. Bush was incommunicado, travelling in a plane. If Haig had read the statute, he would have seen it would have been Tip O'Neil, not Alexander Haig, who would have been in charge.

The other context is when the president knows he is going to go under. Ken Crispell has already discussed that and I don't want to steal any of his thunder. I don't have much to add; I think I'm in complete agreement with him.

On the one hand, we can commend Reagan for actually using the amendment. We can attack him for doing it in a qualified, and ambiguous way, though ultimately history may be kind to that decision. The President's concern apparently was that he did not want to create a precedent. He was willing to rely on the amendment but he did not want to create a precedent of relying on it because he didn't want to bind the hands of his successors. History may be kind to this action and judge it as sensible, but undeniably, he muddled the situation. As you might recall, in his letter, the President wrote that he didn't think the Twenty-fifth Amendment applied to what he was about to do—which was to go temporarily under sedation; but, then, he used all its forms. As a lawyer I would argue that the only available process was to use all the forms of the amendment. The only way he could have transferred power was under the amendment. It was clear enough from the letter that he wanted to transfer power. Despite his disclaimer, I would argue that he did rely on the amendment. But the disclaimer made matters more difficult rather than easier for his successors.

Perhaps—and this is something that I think the majority, and possibly everybody in the Commission, believes—it would be ideal to have this mechanism as an accepted, normal procedure for presidents. There are many health situations for people in that office. The stage of life at which they often reach that office increases the possibility of medical problems that temporarily incapacitates them. Its not just a general anesthesia either, although that is certainly the best example. It is the one that has actually come up. During President Reagan's recent prostate surgery in January—I was out of the country but as I recall he did not have a general but rather a local anesthesia—he was really in no position to act in a crisis. If we could come to accept this procedure as something normal, we would expect a president, when a medical procedure like this one occurs, to rely on it. The procedure would even be pertinent for dental surgery when there is going to be gas. We must accept this normal delegation of authority as temporary and in no way demeaning to the dignity or the symbolic power of the occupant of the office.

That's about all I have to say before answering your questions.

QUESTION: Where do you draw the line? How is a situation where the president has insomnia and he takes sleeping pills related to the Twenty-fifth Amendment?

PROFESSOR STEPHAN: That's a fair question. It is one that was kicked around by the people drafting the Twenty-fifth Amendment. Some thought that sleeping pills fell on one side of the line and general anesthesia on the other. One of the problems is that invocation of the Constitution seems so very powerful and majestic; our initial reactions are not to make it commonplace. On the other hand, there are lots of situations where, whether or not the majesty of the Constitution is invoked, we don't want the president to have ultimate authority. Indeed when he is on sleeping pills, if he is groggy, or it is going to be hard to raise him to consciousness, his staff has to be aware and if necessary the vice president has to be in on things.

During the October War of 1973, there were several moments where our troops were put on general alert and it looked like we were moving toward a confrontation with the Soviets, perhaps a grave one. The accounts that came out of the White House indicate that a committee consisting of Haig, Colby, Kissinger, and Schlesinger pretty much ran the show. They kept Nixon out of it, in this case not so much for health problems, but as a consequence of the other distraction he had. I'm not sure the Twenty-fifth Amendment is automatically the right solution, but I am prepared to say that we can invoke it more comfortably than we have yet done without saying categorically where that line ought to be drawn.

QUESTION: To change the topic somewhat, I have been doing some research on the latter part of the Johnson presidency when Hubert Humphrey was vice president. Humphrey was apparently acting president briefly when Johnson went through an operation. I remember a story in the *Washington Post* to the effect that while Johnson was being operated on, the little man with the "football," the briefcase with the nuclear instructions, moved over to Humphrey's apartment and a special detail of the Secret Service went into motion. However, I never saw any reference to whether there was a letter authorizing this.

PROFESSOR STEPHAN: The amendment did not actually go into effect until 1967 and I don't remember the surgery to which you have alluded exactly. I think it might have been before 1967. Eisenhower's health problems first made presidents aware of potential conflicts until the amendment went into effect. Kennedy and Johnson had a stop-gap procedure modeled on the agreement originally drafted by Bill Rogers for Eisenhower and Nixon, and they may have relied on that.

You have raised a very interesting point. When we talk about presidential authority, the ultimate concern is the "football." One problem that we have had in exploring this area is that the actual chain of command, which we know exists, is classified. We know that there is a procedure to take care of the authority of who calls for the mobilization of nuclear forces—God forbid that ever should be needed—if the president is absent. We do not know what it is because it is classified, and I suppose if any of the members of the Committee did know, they could not reveal it to the other members. So in a sense we have to hedge around the issue that probably is the most important one, the chain of command in the context of a nuclear crisis.

The most we can do—and I think it is important that this Commission is doing so—is to push toward a greater awareness of the health concerns that a president can have. Not simply, for example, going under the knife, but also coming out of general anesthesia. There has now been some talk, including some by the President, that when he resumed power in 1985 and invoked the Twenty-fifth Amendment to take command again, he really wasn't fit. He is now using this as one of the reasons by way of apology for some of the decisions made at that time with respect to the sale of arms to Iran.

I think we've made a contribution to the extent that we can raise awareness about the problems of post-operative effects of surgery and can relate this to whatever chain of command exists for the nuclear codes.

QUESTION: What did the Commission do about psychiatric problems? I'm not thinking only of Wilson's and FDR's problems, but also of those of Lincoln who was allegedly depressed. Certainly Eagleton would have been a risk had he ascended to the presidency, and the same applies to Forrestal because of his paranoia about Russia. Another related problem is alcohol which presumably affected both Grant and Andrew Johnson. How many drinks does it take to incapacitate someone and what did you do about psychiatric care?

PROFESSOR STEPHAN: Before answering, I will add one more to that list; President Kennedy was kept alive by sustained cortisone treatments which also affects the mood. Some people felt that the stress of the Cuban missile crisis generated emotional swings. Although I don't think any of these conditions ever in fact deteriorated into what would be called a "psychiatric problem," there have been background issues involved. I'll punt on the specific question because I'm not a member of the Commission; I'm a counsel. Members of the Commission can address the question of its actions in this area.

I am doing my research on this subject, which is a difficult area. Although I don't have all the facts, I know of a prominent psychiatrist—I think he may be president of the American Psychiatric Association—who gave a speech on psychiatric problems in the presidency. He displayed the political abuses of psychiatry because, on the one hand, he was willing to exculpate Eagleton in spite of his problems, and on the other hand, he was willing to indict Goldwater and Nixon without any direct proof of psychiatric problems. There certainly seemed to be a kind of tendentiousness in this approach. This example isn't typical, and I don't mean to suggest that at all. I just mean to suggest that it's one of the contributing factors to the murkiness. The Commission certainly didn't neglect that and I guess I'll let the other members of the Commission address that.

COMMENT: Although I am not a member of the Commission I'll say two or three things in response to that question. While psychiatric problems have been mentioned and discussed so far within the Commission meetings, I myself think that they have not received the amount of attention they deserve. There has been much more attention placed on physical, orthodox and conventional disabilities, than on psychiatric ones. The very difficulty of the subject and the vagueness of psychiatric illness may turn people away. It is also tied up with another aspect of the problem which the Commission has talked about: the difficulties and practical problems of activating the machinery under Section Four.

In other words, who will ring the alarm? If the president himself doesn't activate the process under Section Three, the Cabinet and the vice president face the difficult situation of deciding who is going to be the first to speak up and say, "The President is out of it." This is a very, real problem. Congress needs to enact a statute that will provide some mechanisms and processes that are currently nonexistent. The problem is to get the vice president off the hook. The solution must not rely on the vice president as the one to take the first step. In the end he must agree to go along, but I think that in real situations, he is going to be extraordinarily reluctant. There is a great fear about a *coup*, but I think the greater fear is the opposite. Reluctance to move when the situation requires action for fear of being suspected of grabbing power is more dangerous.

Cabinet members are also reluctant at times, so some type of process is required. It involves the president's physician and possibly others. Some suggestions propose the creation of an advisory board, not to replace the Cabinet, but to provide a mechanism that can activate it and bring matters to its attention. I think the psychiatric problems as well as the ordinary physical disabilities are very much tied up with processes and procedures for activating the Cabinet under Section Four. This is as much as I can add for the moment. Overall, I agree; the Commission needs to increase its attention on this topic. I'm hoping it will get to it before the work is over.

COMMENT: I would like to correct your previous comment. It wasn't the president of the American Psychiatric Association but someone on the fringe who gave the speech you mentioned before. On the other hand, Milton Greenblat from UCLA presented a paper before the American Psychiatric Association in which he points out the tremendous problem of determining when a president has lost his mind. I agree with Dan; there are times when a physical ailment that doesn't influence judgment or communication can affect an officeholder. The real concern involves judgment and communication, as Bobby Kennedy brought up with Senator Bayh during the hearings.

It is very difficult to determine the way to organize a group that will decide when judgment is impaired. Different groups have suggested the formation of a committee of twelve members who would decide if a president was incompetent or lacked judgment. A serious proposal suggested that five medical leaders and seven government officials could constitute the committee. It seems to me that would bring chaos. I'm sure seven government officials would have problems reaching an agreement and so would five doctors. One of the toughest parts of the whole process is to reach an agreement. There aren't any problems if a person is under anesthesia, suffers a stroke like Wilson, or has a whopping heart attack with cardiac arrest like Eisenhower. The real worry is a condition where the officeholder fades in and out, such as in Alzheimer's disease. Here the victim may feel very competent and *be* very competent but two hours later he may forget the words which he recently spoke.

QUESTION: I'd like to ask a question on another subject. Who has the "football" when the president turns over his duties to the acting president? We can't find out easily. Somebody at one of these conferences told us that during the transfer of power from Nixon to Ford, Jim Schlesinger apparently had the football while Nixon was flying to California. [Editor: Nixon has said he had the football on the flight.] Unless we know what the National Command Authority does, we don't really know who has the football during that period, do we? There is no way our Commission can find out this information unless there is a leak.

PROFESSOR STEPHAN: If we find out, we have learned top secret information. As I said earlier, that really is a fundamental problem and the most important aspect of this whole inquiry. Nixon's case is actually a good example. I was in the government during that summer and I can tell you that toward the end Nixon could not have used the codes even if he had wanted to once a staff decision had been made. This went on for a period of two or three days.

QUESTION: Coming back to the question of who takes the initiative, the historical record probably would prove that almost inevitably the president's chief of staff decides what is to be done. In the cases that I have studied, the chief of staff or some other senior staff person took the initiative in effect and decided what had to be done. In most cases they decided that nothing had to be done. Using the present situation as an example, would Howard Baker have to take the initiative? If he did, would the others probably be willing to go along?

COMMENT: Baker would be more likely to do it than previous chiefs of staff. The great problem is that the palace guard hates to lose the crown. They are going to be reluctant even to hint that anything is wrong until the horse is almost out of the stable.

QUESTION: If Donald Regan had the opportunity, what do you think would have happened?

COMMENT: He'd have taken over himself! I don't think he would have had any doubts about his own ability to do so.
    The point about mental disabilities is excellent because it is probably the weakest part of the Twenty-fifth Amendment. First of all, I can't conceive of a publicly acceptable body. When the question involves determining whether somebody has a mental disability, and the person happens to be the president, it can't stay in the public knowledge very long without chaos erupting.
    I'd like to make one other comment that doesn't offer any solutions, but it will at least contribute something to the discussion. The person I feel sorry for in all of these schemes is the vice president. I've never had any particular love for the office of the vice presidency. Right now I am reading George Mason's biography and one of the ten or twelve reasons he attacked the Constitution was his opposition to the vice presidency. He said it involved a dangerous combination of the legislative and the executive branches of government and he didn't think it was necessary at all. Examination of the behavior of vice presidents will reveal that they are scared to death of this situation. Nixon went up and hid in somebody's house the

first time Eisenhower was ill and he didn't want anybody to find him. He didn't know whether he wanted to be president or not. Vice presidents can't appear to be too eager to want to seize the crown, even though Section Four relies upon initiation of action by the vice president. I think it's a very real problem.

PROFESSOR STEPHAN: During President Wilson's administration Vice President Marshall felt that he did not have the power under the Constitution to do anything about a clearly disabled president. One could say that, on the one hand, Section Four at least now settles that question: The vice president *does* have the power. But, on the other hand, the institutional and political concerns that you've raised pose a very real dilemma.

The vice president can be compared with the head of state of the Soviet Union who has an entirely symbolic position, but unlike the head of state of the Soviet Union, it is possible for the vice president to assume real power. We've seen that happen many times in our lifetimes. Here is where those two aspects of the vice presidency intersect; until he invokes Section Four he is a nonentity, but once it is invoked, he is president, though not permanently as in all other successions.

QUESTION: Since competence and fitness are so difficult to decide, how would you resolve a situation where the president decides that he is competent and others think he is not? This type of situation is frequent at other levels of interaction. Who decides when a president has a temporary disability, either mental or physical? Who decides when he is able to resume his authority?

PROFESSOR STEPHAN: The Amendment has a mechanism but it is not a very happy one. There is a procedure laid out but it is very cumbersome and hard to make stick. In the practical world one hopes to have people around the president who have enough sense of themselves and of duty to country to inform the president first and then tell others. I speak only for myself but I found Dan Ruge, who was President Reagan's physician during his first term, personally very impressive. He is someone who had essentially retired from practice. He was a partner of Royal Davis, Mrs. Reagan's father, and he was selected because he was a senior person whose future did not depend on his appointment as presidential physician. My impression is that he conveyed a sense that if he felt there was something wrong with the President, he knew what he would do. He told us he would first go to Mrs. Reagan and then to William French Smith, not because he was attorney general but because he knew him. This arrangement may not be ideal, it may seem too clannish and involve too many family ties, but at least it is *something*, as opposed to a president's physician who never does anything.

NARRATOR: How about upgrading the idea of the position of presidential physician? As he looked back on it, Dr. Ruge said that the job was a "blue collar job." He met the vice president for the first time the day after the assassination attempt. He wasn't as prominent as we might hope and yet he did say he felt free to call in other medical advisers on the problems he couldn't handle.

COMMENT: We have discussed this in the Commission. I'm obviously biased but I think that the position of presidential physician should be very important. Yet he lacks any authority whatsoever to do anything other than contact the vice president if he thinks the president is ill.

On the other hand, if Congress is involved in the appointment, we run into a real problem with doctor-patient confidentiality. Dr. Lukash who had served several presidents before Dan Ruge believes this might be one way of doing it. Other problems are involved. I recently found out that the president's physician serves at the will of the president and if the president's physician says "You're crazy," the president can say, "No, you are crazy. I'll get another doctor." So even if this became part of a statute or if the position was subject to congressional approval, I don't see it as a final solution to the situation.

COMMENT: All the information that we have gathered for the last two or three years, points toward a reality which unfortunately is not widely recognized: the key role of the president's physician. One of the things that the

Commission's report can do is to make this very clear and offer some recommendations. This applies to both Sections Three and Four of the Amendment. Everybody says, of course, that the decision to transfer power to the vice president is ultimately a political decision. I think that is very true. The problem though is to create a procedure and understanding through which an ultimately political judgment can be expressed in medical terms as well, an aspect that has been missing in the past. There is no body of understanding, custom, nor process in place to guarantee that medical information will be part of the ultimate decision-making process. The president's physician has been treated just as somebody along for the ride, an "intruder" in the White House. Now and then somebody may think of consulting him after decisions have been made. This situation has to change. The physician must be integrated into the process and guaranteed a place, either through internal White House procedures or even through some other statutory process.

The Commission's report, in my opinion, must recommend that the decision-making process will integrate medical judgments, medical opinions and information with the ultimate political judgment about a president's condition and the eventual need to transfer power.

NARRATOR: Would you approve a provision in a statute to establish the right of a physician to disclose information that would affect the interest of the community? Isn't that what Brownell and to some extent Bayh and several others favored? In opposition, others have said that the inclusion of these stipulations may ultimately generate more resistance to the role of the physician.

COMMENT: I don't know if I would go for a statute because it is a fairly heavy-handed way to do something if other options are available. What I do favor is a code of conduct, so to speak, for the president's physician that would spell out fairly specifically the duties and responsibilities of the presidential physician and of the White House staff in relation to the physician. Each incoming president would accept them as a matter of internal operating procedures so everybody would understand them from the outset. All of these aspects have to be spelled out, but I'm not sure I would go as far as supporting a statute.

COMMENT: Let me briefly respond to part of the question. The ABA (American Bar Association) played a really important part in getting this amendment going with Justice Powell. The American Medical Association perhaps could help us. Let me refer to a related topic that is helpful. Last year the Committee on Ethics of the AMA said that it was alright to take away water, fluids and sugar from a dying person. It is an absolutely amazing step, as I'm sure all of you realize, but it now is in print. Literally doctors cannot be sued now, unless they are crazy, for allowing a person to die. I think it is quite possible that we might be able to work with Dr. Schwartz who is a member of the Commission and of the American Medical Association. In political issues of the sort we have discussed the AMA can provide ethical guidelines for the community, specifically in the area of patient-doctor confidentiality.

COMMENT: Future presidents somehow have to agree to use Section Three, not when they are going to take sleeping pills every night but certainly when they are going to have surgery. If the facts as presented in the Iran-Contra hearings prove to be true, it certainly is a dramatic proof that presidents must not be afraid of setting a precedent in doing this.

NARRATOR: Are there any more questions? We think this process is a terribly important part of the whole discussion. Participants in these Forums don't always get their names in print but your questions are fed back to the Commission. We are going to continue doing this. The whole philosophy that undergirds the Miller Center's effort is that if enough people knew about the content and meaning of the Twenty-fifth Amendment, then presidents and presidential staffs would be more willing to consider its use. I think if it were more widely understood, particularly with regard to Section Three, if it were recognized that these procedures are a routine matter and that they have been very carefully thought out, then successive presidents would look on them in a different light. This is the reason why we think these discussions are useful and important. The American Medical Association, the American Bar Association and the League of Women Voters have all offered to find ways of continuing these discussions in other parts of the country in the months and years ahead. So we feel this is a contribution; it's a contribution with people who, as lawyers, legislators, and doctors, have followed the matter closely. It is also a contribution of the University of Virginia staff which has done the research and which has responded to the inquiries such as those our speaker this morning has answered. Thank you all.

MEMORY, INFORMATION AND DENIAL IN PUBLIC LIFE

C. Knight Aldrich, M.D.

NARRATOR: It is a pleasure to introduce today's speaker, Dr. Knight Aldrich. Dr. Aldrich was born in Chicago, and educated at Wesleyan and the Northwestern University Medical School. He began his teaching career at the University of Minnesota Medical School and later went to the University of Chicago as chairman of the Department of Psychiatry. After teaching at the University of New Jersey Medical School in Newark, he came to the University of Virginia as professor of psychiatry and family medicine. He has written several books which include *Psychiatry for the Family Physician, An Introduction to Dynamic Psychiatry,* and *A Case Book for Pastoral Counseling.* He is a fellow of the American College of Psychiatrists, of the American Orthopsychiatric Association, and of the American Psychiatric Association and is a member of the Group for the Advancement of Psychiatry. He has taught abroad, including a year at the University of Edinburgh, and he is widely known and respected in the Charlottesville community. He and his wife Julie have been among the most generous supporters of the Miller Center. He will speak today on memory, information, and denial in public life.

DR. ALDRICH: In contrast with most of my predecessors, I've had no personal connection with presidents; I can't recount anecdotes of the Oval office or Cabinet meetings. Seeing President Carter when he was at the Miller Center was as close as I've ever been to a president. I also hope I won't disappoint you if I don't provide any psychiatric diagnoses of living individuals. All professionals have to be careful with their diagnoses; for instance, you or I can

83

glance at a bridge and say, "That bridge looks as if it's falling down," but an engineer can't say that without examining the bridge, because he is an authority. The same applies to psychiatrists who haven't examined the patient. You can call someone "paranoid" or "senile," but I can't call him that unless I've examined him.

Psychiatrists haven't always paid attention to that rule. About twenty-five years ago an ultra-liberal journal disclosed some alleged information about presidential candidate Goldwater and sent letters to all of us requesting a psychiatric appraisal. Unfortunately a few of my colleagues were unwise enough to respond, which didn't do psychiatry's reputation any good. Psychiatrists should have known better after the experience of a distinguished psychiatrist who made the mistake of diagnosing, from his seat in the courtroom, Whitaker Chambers, who had been called as a witness in the Alger Hiss case. The defense counsel tore him to ribbons for making a diagnosis without examining the patient. So I do not intend to get into that kind of trouble here. Instead I will discuss memory and what happens to memory as we grow older, how changes in memory can affect participation in public life, and how some people unconsciously deny evidence that their memory is failing.

There are three components of memory: the first is the acquisition of information—what is stored in memory; the second part is the retention of information—what is kept in storage; and the third part is the retrieval of information—what can be brought back from storage. All of these are affected by time.

Memory is somewhat like a computer. We hear a lot these days about artificial intelligence, about how the computer can function in ways that are similar to the brain. While there still are ways in which the computer cannot imitate the brain, it comes close with memory. A sophisticated computer has several ways of getting to a particular bit of information so that if the most direct way is blocked, it can find another way. Human memory functions in a similar manner. Fortunately, we have a great deal of memory reserve so it takes a lot of blocking before we run out of alternate pathways and begin to have discernible symptoms of memory loss; in other words, we have more brain cells than we need during most of our lives.

Most of our brain cells are present at birth, and by late childhood we have all that we will ever have, although many of them do not function until adulthood. Nor do they regenerate: once brain cells are gone, they are gone forever, and in contrast to most of the other cells of the body, you can't make new ones. Moreover you lose 100,000 brain cells a day, which means one every second, a thought which can make you nervous, even though you have several billion to lose. As your brain cells disappear, the size of your brain slowly diminishes. By the time you are seventy-five, you have only about fifty-six percent of the functioning brain substance that you had when you were thirty. That's also a little disquieting.

Some of the loss in function may be due more to chemical changes than to a loss of substance. We are not quite sure how much loss is due to what; it is surprising how little we actually know about the brain and memory when we consider how important it is. In any case, the reserve, whether it's chemical or anatomical, gets used up as time goes on. The rate of loss is not the same for everyone; for example, the brain is used up faster when injured, which is why the punch-drunk boxer has severe memory troubles. Diseases, such as strokes, and poisons, such as alcohol, accelerate the loss of memory, but time inevitably wears down even the healthiest brain.

How people react to memory loss depends a great deal on their personalities. There are several ways of measuring personality differences, but the way that I think is most relevant to a discussion of memory is one that the English use called the Maudsley Personality Inventory. The Maudsley Inventory places each individual at a point on a continuum between the perfectionist and the denier.

At one pole is the ultimate perfectionist whose self esteem depends on his accuracy; he has a great need to be absolutely correct in everything for which he is viewed as responsible. How you get to be a perfectionist is another topic, but some people are. They have to do everything themselves because they can't trust other people, to whom they might delegate tasks, to be as perfectionistic as they are. Thus when a perfectionistic wife complains that her

85

husband never does anything around the house, he says, "Why should I? Every time I do something, she does it over to make sure it is done right." So the perfectionist's problem of delegating authority is a problem in private as well as in public life. But even when the perfectionist has done it all himself he may not be quite sure whether it is absolutely right, and this no doubt interferes with his capacity to make decisions expeditiously. In academic life we are familiar with the ABD ("All But Dissertation") Ph.D. student who cannot seem to finish a dissertation because it is never perfect and there is always something else that might be included.

Perfectionists have somewhat unselective memories. They have to remember everything, regardless of its importance; it is hard for them to concentrate on the big picture and forget the trivia. Perfectionists adapt well to jobs with a relatively circumscribed scope, in which they can do it all. The trouble is, they are likely to do it all so well that they get promoted to a job in which they can't do it all. They are the victims of the Peter principle, which says that people get promoted to the level of their incompetence. I knew a perfectionist scientist who was great with the microscope—there's no room for more than one on a microscope—but when he became an administrator, he still had to try to do it all himself. He would do everybody's work all over again, but still couldn't make up his mind, and the files on his desk got higher and higher, and he became more and more miserable until he finally resigned and went back to his lab.

Senator Eugene McCarthy may have been referring to the same phenomenon when not too long ago in this room he suggested that state governors might not be the best candidates for the presidency since that job requires a view that is so much broader than a governor's. More than anyone else a president needs to be able to delegate authority and to trust those to whom he has delegated the authority. He needs to be able to focus on the broad issues and to leave the details to others, and he needs to be able to make decisions expeditiously. If he is too much of a perfectionist he is likely to get bogged down in detail and important decisions will be delayed too long.

The deniers, the people at the other end of the Maudsley scale, are just the opposite. They overdo delegation; when they delegate something, they forget it. They put too much trust in their subordinates, saying to themselves, "Now that I've delegated it, I don't have to worry about it." They tend to deny the importance of any issues in which they are not particularly interested. They are able to deny unpleasantness, either consciously, by avoiding the whole issue, or unconsciously, by forgetting uncomfortable memories or being oblivious to uncomfortable realities.

It is easy for a denier to make decisions, because he looks at only one side of a question; the other side is denied. Since he can easily make decisions which tie the perfectionist in knots, he is much more relaxed. His capacity to deny unpleasantness makes the denier more likely to be optimistic, and therefore reassuring to those around him, while the perfectionist is more likely to be pessimistic. Optimism is a great advantage in a political campaign which relies on brief television appearances in which the candidate has only time to assure us that everything is going to be OK and we don't have to worry about anything. The perfectionist has trouble in that kind of campaign.

The denier has a more selective memory than the perfectionist, since he can push aside or repress troublesome memories. He also has a tendency to fill in the blanks with what is less troublesome, so he is less precise and more likely to distort. The distortion is usually unconscious, or it would not be convincing, so the denier really believes in the distorted reality that emerges from his computer. He therefore tends to be a good raconteur, since he can easily adapt reality or history to the story he wants to tell, while the perfectionist is usually not as good a raconteur, although a better historian. The denier is seldom motivated to get into graduate studies, and if he does he is likely not to persist, so those of us in academic settings are more likely to see perfectionists than deniers. The denier's overdelegation, avoidance of unpleasant present realities, and distortion of past realities interfere with his capacity for objective leadership, and can create more serious problems when the stakes are high than when they are relatively low.

Perfectionists and deniers are at opposite poles of this personality continuum; most of us are somewhere in between. Ideally a president, or person in any other high executive office, should be in between the poles. He or she should be able to remember in some detail, but should not try to remember everything. He should be able to delegate, but also should recognize where the buck stops. He should be able to decide with dispatch, but not impulsively.

Memory loss affects the executive abilities of anyone, whether he is a perfectionist, a denier, or in between. What happens when the memory computer is damaged? As I said before, memory loss can occur from injury, poison, or disease, although when we think about memory defects, we usually think first of *Alzheimer's disease*. Alzheimer was a German doctor who in 1907 reported a case of a person who had lost his memory at the age of fifty-one. He called this condition *pre-senile dementia*; others later called it "Alzheimer's disease." At the time doctors believed that *senile dementia*, or severe loss of memory and brain function, was inevitable in old age. I remember my professor saying to us, after demonstrating a patient with senile dementia, "This is what will happen to all of you if you live long enough and if nothing else gets you first." Alzheimer believed that his patients were developing senile dementia at an early age.

The idea that everybody would eventually become senile and demented persisted until five or ten years ago. Since then there has been extensive research into Alzheimer's disease, which is now viewed as a separate disease, occurring either early or late in old age, and including both Alzheimer's pre-senile dementia and senile dementia.

Dementia is no longer perceived as an inevitable accompaniment of aging. The popular view now is that aged people are just as competent as they ever were; they are just a little bit slower to retrieve information, and even the slowness is minimized. Thus a neurologist writes, "[Memory] changes attributable to aging alone are minimal. The mode in recent memory is usually normal, however the speed of processing information or retrieving memory slows in patients older than seventy years. Learning capacity and the ability to make new memories also decrease." Note that in his first sentence the neurologist minimizes the slowness as really not a defect. This minimization is part of an effort to dissociate the Alzheimer's patient altogether from the rest of the aged, and to consider the rest of the aged normal.

This effort is encouraged by the militancy of the senior citizen lobby, which has also contributed to the steady rise in retirement age. The rise in retirement age still excludes, fortunately I believe, pilots, firemen, and the police, all of whom must be able to respond quickly to emergencies. Pilots, firemen, and policemen, as well as others whose jobs require rapid storage and retrieval of information, cannot afford to operate with slowed-down memory computers, while most of the rest of us are not seriously handicapped.

The extent of the handicap caused by the slowing of any bodily function is determined by the setting as, for example, in the case of the light reflex. The light reflex is the eye's response to a sudden increase or decrease in the amount of light, as when a bright lamp is turned on or off in a dark room. Some of you who have reached my age have probably noticed that your light reflexes have slowed down; you may have noticed this slowing in the setting of the movies. When I go into a theatre which is all dark except for the screen, it takes me a while before I can find an empty seat. If I don't want to sit on somebody's lap, I wait in the rear until my light reflex responds and I can see which seats are occupied. That wasn't the case when I was younger, but it is not too inconvenient; after a while I can find a seat as well as I ever could. The slowing of my light reflex is only significant in a setting in which a rapid response is required, as when I am driving a car at night. With my slow light reflex, it takes me a while to respond when oncoming headlights flash into my eyes. By the time I've responded to the lights it is dark again, and I need to respond the other way in order to see the road. Slowing of the light reflex is only dangerous in settings in which when a rapid response is required; in the same way, slowing of information storage and retrieval is only dangerous in settings in which a rapid response is required.

As I said before, the number of everyone's brain cells diminishes gradually, and there is also a change in our brain chemistry as we get older. We have enough reserves so that these changes are usually not apparent until the early seventies or thereabouts. There are substantial individual differences in the rate at which we dip into our reserves, so that some people (who do not have Alzheimer's disease) begin to have recent memory troubles in their sixties and others do not begin to notice it until their eighties, or even later. We are reminded in this room of the late Dumas Malone, who attended many of these sessions until well into his nineties and always asked the last question. His memory was extraordinarily well preserved, but his eyes and ears were not, illustrating how aging progresses at different rates in different organ systems.

Eventually, though, our brains' reserves are used up while the chemistry changes, our acquisition and retrieval of information become slower, and our retention of information becomes weaker. These changes are particularly evident for what is called "new memory," or memory for recent events. Early, or "remote" memory and immediate memory both hold up better than recent memory so you can remember what happened a few years ago or a few minutes ago, but not what occurred in between. You say to yourself, "I am pleased to meet you, Ken Thompson," and think, "of course I will remember him." But half an hour later you have lost it. You see Ken, but because you haven't time to wait for the slower retrieval process to bring his name back, you say, "Your name is. . .?," and he says, "Ken Thompson." Then, in order to regain your self esteem, you reach back into your remote memory and say, "Oh yes, I remember a Thompson back in sixth grade. His name was Sam. . ." and so on into the past, because that lets you think, "My memory isn't gone. I can remember way back to sixth grade." Your capacity rapidly to retrieve information that was stored earlier in your life, when your reserves were greater, is retained longer than your capacity to store and retrieve recent information.

My grandfather enjoyed telling a particular story of early Chicago politics. It was an interesting story the first time he told it, but he kept telling it, and it became less interesting with successive repetitions. His intact remote memory let him remember the story, but his defective recent memory did not let him remember that he had already told the story, so he was not aware that he was repeating himself. Grandfather also became a lot more resistant to change in his old age, in part because he could remember the old days better and was more comfortable with old memories.

The tendency of older people to lose their recent memory has recently been labeled "benign senescent forgetfulness." I particularly like the adjective "benign," which contrasts nicely with the "malignant" forgetfulness of Alzheimer's disease. Alzheimer's disease usually progresses rapidly, while benign senescent forgetfulness, happily for those of us in the "senescent" years, is very slow to progress. But it progresses nevertheless, and it can be depressing, as depressing as any of the infirmities of aging, especially if one is an intellectual, and still more so if one is a perfectionist.

To avoid these depressed feelings, we try, unconsciously, to deny or to rationalize their cause. Thus an eminent scholar in his seventies said to me after I had described benign senescent forgetfulness, "I don't see it in myself; it hasn't happened to me. My memory is as good as or better than it ever was." But a few minutes later, when we were talking about another meeting, he uncharacteristically said, "I had better put it down in my notebook; I'm so busy these days that I might forget it." Our efforts to deny are supported by the strength of our remote memory, of our vocabulary, which holds up well, and of our immediate memory. We also use such rationalizations as: "I've always had a poor memory for names," or "I only forget trivia." Denial and rationalization protect our self-esteem, and they are innocuous defenses so long as they do not stand in the way of compensating for the memory loss. Thus my scholar friend could deny his forgetfulness and rationalize his use of his notebook with impunity so long as he kept using the notebook.

The perfectionist, who needs to be 100% accurate in his information and finds it difficult to deny or to rationalize, becomes aware early of beginning memory defects, even before they can be identified by testing, and then is likely to become depressed. We have long known

91

that people who are perfectionists are vulnerable to depression in what we call the "involutional years," the fifties or sixties, and it may be that the beginning loss of memory contributes to the depression. That may well have been the case with Secretary of Defense James Forrestal, whose severe depression ended tragically with suicide.

Benign senescent forgetfulness isn't as obvious in the denier, who has always been able to push disturbing things aside. He pushes the early signs of memory loss aside, so that when it finally increases to the point that he no longer can deny it, it seems to be a sudden and not a gradual loss. Even then he finds it easier to deny its significance and turn his attention to other concerns than is the case with the perfectionist, who cannot protect himself from the evidence of his loss of function.

The significance of benign forgetfulness or slow information retrieval in public life depends on how much the particular public servant's role requires an immediate and knowledgeable response to emergencies. Justice Holmes is often cited as an example of someone who retained effectiveness into his nineties; the judicial branch, however, can tolerate memory deficiencies because a justice has clerks and notes, and has adequate time to complete his tasks. So in the judicial branch loss of recent memory can progress a fair distance before serious problems emerge.

Justice Holmes told an anecdote about Justice Robert Greer, an 1846 Polk appointee, who by 1869, when he was seventy-six years old, had become unable to do his job because of severe memory loss. His disability was tolerated until a crisis arose when the Court was split four to four on a crucial issue. At that time a delegation, including Justice Stephen Field, was sent to Justice Greer to advise him to retire. Thirty years or so later Justice Field also suffered severe memory loss, and the rest of the Court decided that he ought to retire. Again they sent a delegation which began by asking Justice Field if he recalled participating in Justice Greer's retirement. Light returned to Justice Field's somewhat vacant eyes as he pulled himself together and said, "Yes, and a dirtier day's work I never did in my life." According to Justice Holmes, the delegation retreated in confusion.

C. Knight Aldrich, M.D.

The legislative branch is larger than the Court and seldom acts in haste, and some members, such as former Senator Claude Pepper, have apparently been effective into their eighties. So far forgetfulness does not appear to have adversely affected legislative function, although it may in the future. Increased longevity and the increased expense of defeating an incumbent may lead to an increased proportion of octogenarians in the legislature, with a consequent increased resistance to change, especially if senior members dominate key committees.

The requirements for quick information retrieval are much greater in the executive branch, especially for the president. The president must be able to adapt rapidly to emergencies and to make fast decisions. He has the "football"; he is the one who can press the button, and in that situation he can't rely on cue cards or props to help him. Briefings before meetings with congressional committees, the news media, or heads of state help, although the superiority of immediate over recent memory may give him a false sense of security; immediately after the briefing he can recall the material better than he can later during the meeting. Over-learning may bolster the memory somewhat, but it requires both time and awareness that it is needed, neither of which may be available. Neither briefing nor overlearning, neither cue cards nor prompters can help in the unexpected crisis situation when the president's decision-making depends on his rapid retrieval of a vast amount of information, most of which has been recently stored.

Most executive positions in industry and in academic life still have set retirement ages. You can stay on as professor but you must leave your department chair at a certain age. Why does not the same apply to executives in government, whose capacity for informed and expeditious decision-making is so crucial for the rest of us? The Founding Fathers set a lower age limit of thirty-five, but I suspect it didn't occur to them to set an upper limit, since two hundred years ago not many people survived to old age. Furthermore, there was little need for emergency decisions in those days because of the slowness of communication. When communication is slow, slow information retrieval or

93

loss of recent memory isn't as important for a chief executive as it is when communication is immediate.

William Henry Harrison at sixty-seven was the oldest president we had until Eisenhower, so we haven't had as much experience with older chief executives as some other nations have had. Adenauer is often used as an example of an effective old head of state; Deng may now be another, and for a while Churchill certainly seemed to be effective, although as time went on, he too had trouble with his memory. Mao apparently had memory problems, as have many of the Soviet First Secretaries before Gorbachev, who is relatively young and, not surprisingly, less conservative and more responsive to current realities than his predecessors. There are also the sad and tragic examples of Hindenburg and Petain to demonstrate the importance of intact memory in a chief of state.

Most of today's complex emergencies have time-pressures built in. Birren, reporting his studies of aging, observes that the elderly are at their worst when difficult material and time pressures combine. Consider the consequences of an elderly individual with benign forgetfulness who had to cope with a Cuban missile crisis, or with a Strangelove scenario, or with an accidental discharge of a nuclear armed missile. Imagine him dealing with blackmail by someone like Gadhafi or Idi Amin equipped with nuclear weapons. Think of all the potential crises in Nicaragua, in Afghanistan, in Lebanon, and in the Persian Gulf. Even a peaceful situation can require the kind of emergency mobilization of recent information which the elderly no longer can carry out. Suppose that there is a Chernobyl-like disaster in Texas with the wind blowing south. In all these situations the president must have the capacity to acquire, store, and retrieve both new and old information rapidly and accurately.

Even a relatively young president may not be smart enough, or informed enough, or even inclined to become informed enough to cope with emergencies, but there is no need to compound the problem with memory deficiencies as well. The Twenty-fifth Amendment, which was set up to deal with presidential incapacity, might well be adequate in the kind of acute incapacity that results from an assassination attempt or a surgical condition. It is doubtful, however, whether the amendment can deal with chronic, insidiously developing conditions, especially conditions not acknowledged by the president, and which may be disguised or concealed for various reasons. As Robins and Rothschild point out, people close to the president often have strong motivations to limit public knowledge of presidential disability. They also have a great capacity for insulating their leader from evaluation by the press, by the political opposition, and even by the president's allies in the cabinet and Congress.

A medical judgment may be, and has been, modified by political considerations, often with honorable motives. The president's staff may believe, as did Woodrow Wilson's physician, that the president's health requires the continued challenge of office. The staff may believe, like Grover Cleveland's or Franklin Roosevelt's intimates, that the well-being of the country requires their silence; they believe that their man sick is better for the world than another man healthy. Or their motives may be other than honorable; to be in a president's inner circle as his adviser, physician, or appointment secretary is to have prestige, power, and even profit, and people who attain such positions are often disinclined to jeopardize this.

Even so, the Twenty-fifth Amendment does not cover benign senescent forgetfulness, which is after all not an illness. So what is the solution? There is no fool-proof answer, but an important step would be another constitutional amendment setting an upper age limit, perhaps seventy, in addition to the lower age limit to candidates for the presidency. Even that would permit a president to be in office until seventy-four, but at least no more.

In summary, then, the benign senescent forgetfulness that inevitably catches up with the elderly limits executive capacity to respond to emergencies. This limitation is sufficiently dangerous to justify consideration of a constitutional amendment to set an upper as well as a lower age for presidential candidates.

Executive function is also handicapped by perfectionism and by its opposite, a predilection for the use of the psychological mechanism of denial. Perfectionists are susceptible to depression and deniers to unrealistic avoidance in the face of benign forgetfulness.

QUESTION: There is an ancient folk wisdom that says that the aged are wise. Do you think there is any evidence that there is a plus as well as a minus to the aging process, although our memory fails? Do we gain as well as lose something?

DR. ALDRICH: I hope that there are some gains, since I'm in that age group. It's a little hard to pin it down, though, as to just what those gains are. Experience clearly helps one to appraise situations, but there comes a time when experience gets counter-balanced by memory deficiencies. I suspect that the advantages of aging for the presidency have been exhausted by the age of seventy.

QUESTION: This is another aspect of the last question. Do the other faculties in the brain, such as reasoning and creativity, decline with memory or do they stay?

DR. ALDRICH: Some do, some don't. I believe that nobody ever did the work for which he won the Nobel prize in mathematics after the age of twenty-eight; mathematical creativity seems to diminish early. On the other hand, Richard Strauss wrote tone poems in his eighties, so creativity's survival varies according to the area. I'm not suggesting that the age of seventy should be an age for retirement from all positions, just positions with a crucial need to be able to respond rapidly to emergencies. We know little enough about memory, but even less about creativity.

COMMENT: Perhaps in males the lower level of testosterone with advancing years has a positive effect on judgment.

DR. ALDRICH: You may be right, but I suspect that that happens earlier than seventy.

QUESTION: Dr. Aldrich, is there any relationship between the activity of the mind during its working years and the loss of memory? Does an active professor, doctor, or mathematician, retain memory longer?

DR. ALDRICH: I think that the harder you work to compensate for the effects of aging on memory, the better you can handle the demands on your memory. For instance, if you are in a field in which you are trained to look at data critically, you are more prepared to use props and devices to compensate as you begin to see your memory slipping, so that your functioning memory is better sustained. Whether the actual memory is better preserved is hard to say. On the other hand, the person with an active mind is losing more of what is important to him, and so may give up, become depressed, and do less to compensate.

QUESTION: I would find it difficult to vote for a compulsory retirement bill for presidents, although I wouldn't have any difficulty in voting for one for firemen and policemen. Your example of Adenauer makes a case against age limits. The Germans really needed someone with his wisdom; he seemed to be healthy; and for a period of ten years he made an enormous difference. I would also not vote for an age limit for jurists because, as you pointed out, they have clerks, and they can take their time. The current court is the oldest one in history; no one wants to step down, but they can do their job, and that may be true of other professions. What I am really asking you is: would we perhaps deprive ourselves of someone like Holmes as president if we had an upper age limit?

DR. ALDRICH: I think you do risk losing an Adenauer or someone of his stature, but I think that risk is more than offset by the risks of a Hindenburg. It's a question of probabilities. When you talk about an Adenauer, you are talking about an exception, at the far end of the curve. In the same way you could say that you don't want to retire all the professors in this university because of the example of Dumas Malone. I think the risk that you undertake in sanctioning the election of elderly people who, with few exceptions, are impaired in their ability to deal with emergencies in order to avoid the loss of an exceptional individual is too great.

QUESTION: Is it possible to fake benign senescent forgetfulness if it would be useful to you? And how serious is it?

DR. ALDRICH: I think you can fake memory loss when it is convenient for you.   If you normally deny or repress unpleasantness it might come quite naturally, and you can make a virtue of it. The real problem of benign senescent forgetfulness is that it is not voluntary, and that you do not have control over it.   Forgetful people, especially if they are deniers, may without realizing it confabulate, or construct substitute stories to replace what they have forgotten.

QUESTION: It seems to me you've given us a good view of the state of the art at this moment.   I think your point about the presidency and old age is a good one, but we might not have to confront the problems this involves if the new biology really works out. The progress which has been made   in   neuro-biology   is   frightening   and   almost unbelievable. We have learned an incredible amount about the brain in the last five years with the new tools we have for studying the brain.   With magnetic resonance imaging, for example, we are going to study the chemistry in the memory center.   I think fifty years from now, if we make as much progress in neurobiology as we have made in cardiology and high blood pressure, we will be in a position to look at a candidate's CAT scan and decide on his fitness for the presidency.

DR. ALDRICH: First, you have more confidence than I have in the physician, both his capacity and his willingness to blow the whistle on his patient when his patient is headed for the highest office in the land.   Second, I think fifty years is a long time to go without any insurance against the kind of emergency that I have been talking about.   Finally, although I recognize that we are rapidly learning a lot more about the chemistry and structure of the brain, I am not sure that we are close to using it to prevent forgetfulness. We've also learned a lot about cancer, but we are still a long way from preventing it.

QUESTION: What is the relationship between memory and that imponderable we call "judgment?" If memory is a component in the decision-making process, how much weight should be placed on memory in relation to judgment?

DR. ALDRICH: Judgment certainly develops as one gets older, but its exercise requires a balanced diet of data. If your data is biased towards old memory and against new memory, it doesn't matter how good your potential judgment is; you are still going to have a hard time using it. It is important to make sure that new as well as old memories are represented in the decision-making process.

QUESTION: What would you think if a president in office, or before he ran for office, were required to take some kind of a mental status examination given by a panel of psychiatrists who are selected by the opposition party?

DR. ALDRICH: Robinson and Rothschild have suggested something similar, but I see too many barriers. First, psychiatrists are much better at diagnosing and treating than at predicting psychiatric problems, and the panel presumably is asked to predict. But even diagnosis and treatment require the patient's motivation; the individual well enough to be in this position is well enough to conceal any minor problems from me or my colleagues. Even memory tests, unless the defect is obvious, are hard to evaluate.

But suppose I have examined nominee Jones; picture me on this panel, with a deciding vote. I report my view that nominee Jones is unfit, based on a long, complicated evaluation with, inevitably, a lot of qualifications. Is anyone going to take this seriously, or seriously enough to determine Mr. Jones' candidacy, especially if I have been selected by the opposition party? Even if, as in the Eagleton case, I am asked if an episode of depression and shock treatment should exclude him, I would have to answer in probabilities. No thank you, I don't want the job, and I think you would have a lot of trouble getting a psychiatric panel's findings accepted.

A problem that is related to memory has to do with mental illness in high office, particularly paranoid disturbances. The depression that cost James Forrestal's life in 1949 was accompanied by paranoid delusions—false beliefs about communists and Russians in the government. Had Forrestal been a little more advanced in his career, he might have been considered as a running mate for Roosevelt in 1944 instead of Truman when the more conservative Democrats were desperately trying to get rid of Henry Wallace; he was in fact considered as Truman's running mate in 1948. If he had been picked and had become president and had then become depressed and paranoid, his decisions could well have resulted in war before anyone could have intervened. I believe that the possibility of presidential mental illness as well as the possibility of presidential memory defects must be given serious consideration, and I am not at all sure that either the Twenty-fifth Amendment or a qualifying mental status examination can provide the nation with adequate protection.

NARRATOR: What we have opened up here with Dr. Aldrich is the first discussion on mental capacity as an aspect of presidential disability and the Twenty-fifth Amendment. We will continue this discussion with Dr. Norman Knorr in our next Forum. We thank Dr. Aldrich very much for a remarkably clear and well-organized presentation on an immensely complex subject.

PSYCHOLOGICAL CONSIDERATIONS

Norman J. Knorr, M.D. and Daniel Harrington, M.D.

When a person's sense of security is threatened, psychic stress is felt, and a psychological reaction occurs. The reactions to this intrapersonal stress are usually evidenced by withdrawal of the individual with an expression of hurt feelings, or anxiety with aggressive overtones which may be represented by verbal and physical outbursts. These reactions are normal and usually of brief duration. During the reaction period, from seconds to days, the individual's judgment may be temporarily clouded and decisions hastily made which are not always in the best interest of the individual or significant others. While these normal reactions are of little consequence in everyday life, they may lead to behavior which brings discomfort to others. Usually the instigator of the incident, the stress reactor, appears immature and rather foolish.

If the president of the United States exhibits even these normal emotional reactions to stress he is at risk to receive public criticism. If his reactions become commonplace, he may lose the esteem of his supporters and the electorate. The president receives overt and covert messages that his lifelong adaptation to stress is no longer permissible. Since the emotional reactions are not available for elimination by self control, the obvious management of the problem is to limit the president's public appearances, whenever possible, in which his sense of security is threatened. For the sake of the president's mental health and well-being, however, it is essential that negative emotions find adequate expression. The buildup of stress can be overwhelming when the workday and responsibilities of the president are considered, and if emotions are not discharged in a rational manner it can lead to the development of a variety of psychological disorders.

The president's family, associates, friends, and physician, by allowing and encouraging the expression of emotions, in private, can be helpful in bringing relief of emotional distress and promoting sustained mental health. If the mix of persons surrounding the president is not emotionally supportive the development of psychological disorder of some kind is possible, even probable.

Provided below is a discussion of the psychological disorders, and physical disorders causing psychological impairment, that can provoke disability in the presidential age group. Not only should we be concerned about the direct effect of the illness but we must also consider the president's reaction to the development of illness, the threat of loss of health and the stresses associated with the office of the president.

Physical Illness and the Resulting Psychological Function

The development of an illness can have significant impact on the physical and psychological functioning of the individual. Every illness results in a psychological change for the patient and each patient must readjust his self image from one of a healthy individual to one that is less than before. This reassessment is a result of the individual's ability to look at himself in terms of loss and to form a new realistic self image based on an awareness of losses, limitations and acceptance of a new level of functioning. This process may be short lived if the patient has a minor illness where restoration to health occurs. Minor illnesses such as flu or low back strain may temporarily impair the performance of an individual resulting in loss from work, social impairment and psychological stress. Minor medical illnesses in the president are generally not publicly reported; but, he is not unlike the rest of the population where temporary impairment may occur as a result of the illness itself, or from prescribed medication or the psychological stress related to the illness.

More severe adjustments may occur after the development of more severe chronic illnesses such as diabetes, hypertension, renal failure, cancer and heart disease. However, if the illness is long standing and a permanent disability results, then the patient must recalibrate to a new level of physiological and psychological functioning. An example of an illness that could interfere with the physical and mental stability of the president would be the development of renal failure. This medical condition is associated with impaired clearance of metabolic wastes by the kidney causing uremia which may result in a significant impairment in stamina, concentration, and at times confusion and delirium. In severe cases dialysis may be needed to maintain life. Another example that may cause physical and psychological impairment for the president would be the sequela of a heart attack. A heart attack damages the heart muscle and can result in intermittent periods of chest pain, shortness of breath and decreased stamina. This condition may result in a permanent disability, the chronic need for medication and severe curtailment in activities. Common responses to this condition are fear, anxiety and depression. These responses are particularly common in those individuals who have been hard driving executives.

The president as with other people who face chronic illness responds to the illness in a number of ways. Grief, fear, anxiety, helplessness, hopelessness and guilt are common emotions that a person may feel when faced with the prospects of living with a chronic illness. How a person responds to the illness is determined by which coping mechanisms that person uses when stressed. Everyone uses coping mechanisms to deal with problems of living. These coping mechanisms include denial, anger, anxiety, depression, regression, isolation, intellectualization, blaming and acceptance. Certain coping mechanisms are less adaptive than others in helping the person come to grips with an illness and going on with his life. For example, regression and isolation are maladaptive and cause many difficulties for the individual who uses these coping mechanisms. Not everyone can achieve a level of acceptance where dealing with a major illness does not significantly alter a person's ability to effectively deal with the stresses of the job, family and the illness. Consequently, a president who must deal with an acute or chronic illness could have psychological impairment that would interfere with decision making ability, leadership qualities, and relationship with world, political and business leaders. The results could be devastating. Both physiological and psychological health are imperative to the effective leadership that the presidency demands.

Some illnesses may develop abruptly resulting in significant and immediate disability for the president. The illness could acutely disable the president but have varying degrees of recovery. Examples would include a cerebral vascular accident (stroke), primary or metastatic brain tumor, cardiac arrhythmia and cardiac arrest with resuscitation. The following examples discuss possible scenarios that could occur during the president's term in office.

Cerebral vascular disease may cause several clinical conditions ranging from transient ischemic attack which causes temporary paralysis, aphasia, confusion, loss of eyesight with usually full recovery. This may be the harbinger of a future devastating stroke. This transient cerebral insult could result in brief impairment in the patient in terms of physical ability as well as behavioral and emotional stability. Recovery can be complete but the illness raises issues about the future of the president's health and future liability and competency. In fact, historical sources have concluded that President Woodrow Wilson had transient ischemic attacks before his major stroke. The warnings went unheeded and the President suffered a major stroke with only partial recovery that left him and his administration disabled.

A severe cerebral vascular accident or stroke often results in paralysis, aphasia, depression, confusion and even death. Recovery after the stroke can be variable with most people having some residual dysfunction. If the president had a stroke, in a very short period of time this medical condition could leave the president physically or mentally incapable of leading the country. This illness usually would be apparent and critical decisions would have to be made regarding the president's abilities to perform his duties. The decision to invoke Section 4 of the 25th Amendment to the Constitution of the United States would need to be considered. The presidency of Woodrow Wilson is an example of how a stroke might impair the abilities of the president to carry out his duties. After President Wilson's stroke much of the governing of the country was believed to be carried out by Mrs. Wilson and the presidential advisers. Many examples have been presented that supported the belief that President Wilson had periods of irritability, unpredictability and confusion following an incomplete recovery from the stroke and resulted in severe impairment in the President and his advisers to carry out their plan for governing the country. If this occurred today difficult issues would arise if the president had a partial recovery. Questions regarding the issues of competency, ability to lead and physical disability would have to be addressed. With the exposure of the presidency to the scrutiny and eyes of the public and press in today's world it would seem impossible to have an internal cover-up of such an illness.

Another illness that would present difficulties would be the scenario in which the president developed a primary or metastatic brain tumor. Small tumors may be located in an area of the brain where obvious physical or mental impairment would not be overtly noticeable. However, small tumors in the temporal or frontal lobes could interfere with the president's concentration, decision making abilities, and result in emotional lability and unpredictability far earlier than other overt neurological findings, thereby making the determination of inability to serve difficult. In addition, inappropriate affect, mania, depression, and psychosis could result from this type of lesion. Many brain tumors grow quickly resulting in paralysis, seizures, loss of consciousness without marked behavioral symptoms making the physical disability the determining factor as to whether the president can effectively serve his country.

Not only can many medical illnesses affect the brain but many commonly used medications result in brain dysfunction. All medications have the potential to cause side effects and each individual may respond to a medication in an idiosyncratic way. In fact, estimates report that 5% of all hospital admissions are the result of drug reactions. As a person ages the odds increase that a medication will be necessary to treat some medical problem. Consequently, the likelihood exists that side effects will occur because of the older patient's lower tolerance to medication. In addition, polypharmacy is a major problem in the older population because of the need for multiple medications to treat a variety of medical problems. This increases the chances that drug interactions will occur.

It is widely known that certain medications are more likely to cause emotional or behavioral disorders than others. These include some antihypertensive medications, steroids, antiulcer medications (Cimetodine and Ranitidine), analgesic medications (narcotics and nonsteroidal antiinflammatory agents), sedatives (benzodiazepines and barbiturates), and anticonvulsants.

Hypertension or high blood pressure is a common medical problem that affects approximately 20% of the population. Thus, it would not be uncommon for the president to have hypertension and be under treatment for this common medical condition. A number of the medications used for the treatment of hypertension can result in the development of the clinical syndrome of depression.

The class of drugs called the B Blockers are often used to treat hypertension. Examples include propranolol, metoprolol and nadolol {to name a few}. In approximately 10% of all cases where these drugs are used a depression develops. In addition to these antihypertensive agents, alpha methyl dopa and reserpine are also frequent offenders but are less used at this time to treat hypertension and are thus less likely to cause difficulties.

The syndrome of depression that develops may range from a mild dysphoria to a full blown major depressive episode with altered sleep, social withdrawal, impaired concentration, inability to make decisions, suicidality and hallucinations. Obviously, if this condition were to occur it would have a significant affect on the ability of a president to carry out the affairs of state.

The corticosteroids are another class of drugs that commonly cause behavioral and emotional disorders. This class of drugs has many uses ranging from the treatment of asthma and rheumatoid arthritis to inflammatory bowel disease and malignancy. In addition, they are used for replacement therapy in those patients who have lost the ability to produce their own hormone such as in Addison's

Norman J. Knorr, M.D. and Daniel Harrington, M.D.

Disease or self induced suppression of the adrenal gland secondary to chronic use of steroids. Behavioral problems most often occur with higher doses of these medications but have also been reported with moderate doses. Up to 24 percent of patients receiving these drugs report some behavioral symptoms. The clinical syndromes reported to occur with the use of these hormones include: psychosis with delusions, hallucinations and paranoia; delirium with confusion, hallucinations and paranoia; mood disorders ranging from mania with grandiosity and increased energy to depression with suicidal ideation. Sudden withdrawal of steroids where chronic use has occurred may result in adrenal insufficiency and causes agitation, insomnia, delirium and depression. In addition, abrupt withdrawal of the exogenously ingested hormone may be life threatening in those patients who have suppression of the adrenal gland or who have Addison's Disease. President Kennedy developed Addison's Disease early in his career and took corticosteroids for many years without known behavioral difficulty.

Use of medications such as benzodiazepines, barbiturates or other nonbarbiturate sedative hypnotic gents for anxiety and insomnia, or the use of narcotic analgesic agents for pain present several problems when considering factors that may result in the disability of the president. Many of these medications are commonly prescribed and could conceivably be used by the president either acutely or chronically. All of these medications have effects on brain tissue because that is the mechanism by which they provide relief from anxiety, pain or insomnia. However, this particular quality of the drugs also causes problems in terms of addiction, impaired judgment, depression and behavioral disinhibition.

The benzodiazepines are some of the most commonly prescribed drugs in the United States and have many beneficial uses including the treatment of generalized anxiety disorders and panic disorders. Unfortunately, these drugs are often used inappropriately and are also overprescribed and frequently result in abuse and addiction in patients. The reaction of patients to these drugs is similar to alcohol and provide the user with a sense of well-being and relief from anxiety and fear. However, this can provide a false sense of security to the user and may impair reaction time and judgment. Many reports of benzodiazepine associated amnesia have been published in which individuals have interacted with others and made decisions where, after recovery, the user has no recollection of his actions during drug usage. These drugs are often abused and result in a tremendous amount of disability. It is possible that given the stresses and pressures of the job, the president could at some time during his presidency use this type of medication resulting in impaired decision making.

The chronic use of all of these medications may result in addiction and with this the possibility that withdrawal could occur if the medications were abruptly stopped. With chronic use of these drugs, tolerance develops resulting in increasing amounts of the medication to achieve the same effects that were experienced on a smaller dosage. Addiction occurs with the repeated daily use of a medication of the long term (weeks to months) chronic use of the drug. Upon abrupt discontinuation of the drug, withdrawal syndromes may develop that range from insomnia, irritability, decreased concentration and anxiety to physical instability with seizures, hallucinations and even death.

Alcoholism

Alcoholism is another common disease that could likely cause disability in the president. Alcohol is the favorite American drug of abuse with approximately 10-15 million Americans suffering from addiction. It is a socially acceptable drug that has widespread use and abuse in our culture and has even affected the presidency. Several previous presidents are believed to have had alcohol addiction including Warren Harding, Ulysses Grant and, it is said, Andrew Jackson.

Alcohol is a drug that is so prevalently available that problems may insidiously develop. As the need for relief from the pressures of living becomes paramount, the individual addicted to alcohol needs increasing amounts of alcohol to provide for continued relief from the stresses. This results in increased use of alcohol such that the individual may find himself drinking daily or needing alcohol

Norman J. Knorr, M.D. and Daniel Harrington, M.D.

prior to important meetings or as a relaxant after a long day's work. Soon the person craves alcohol and the physiologic and psychologic need for alcohol is established resulting in addiction.

Alcohol is a brain tissue depressant that results in a false sense of well being, sedation and reduces anxiety. These feelings occur with varying amounts of alcohol, depending on the presence or absence of tolerance. With larger amounts of alcohol the individual develops impaired coordination and judgment, slurred speech, disinhibition, blackouts and amnesia. Alcoholism can develop in any individual who uses the drug daily or intermittently if large amounts are consumed. The danger of alcoholism lies in the fact that denial is the cornerstone of the illness. Consequently, individuals suffering from the disease do not realize that they have a problem and believe that they can stop drinking at any time. Alcoholism causes a tremendous amount of economic, personal and health loss.

Most presidents consume alcohol as a pattern that was learned earlier in life. Frequent alcohol use may occur during the presidency in association with entertaining and as a means to relax after a difficult day. The president, like the rest of the population, has a significant chance of using alcohol as a sedative and relaxant. It is not feasible to consider the possibility that abuse and addiction to the drug could occur. This type of problem could go unnoticed because of the degree of alcohol use that occurs in those around the president. Obvious impairment may come late in the course of the illness but it is probable that the person abusing alcohol may frequently make poor judgment despite the surface appearance that all is well. The president could be in this category and could be under the influence of the drug when making important decisions.

It is not known to what degree alcohol is used in the White House. During the Carter presidency alcohol was probably less used than at the present time. In recent years the admission of alcoholism and drug abuse by the First Lady, Betty Ford, has publicly brought to light the fact that alcoholism can be hidden for a long period of time. Alcoholism in the First Lady was not commonly recognized at the time of her husband's tenure. Alcoholism has no doubt played a part in the presidency many times

109

during the last 211 years but has largely gone unrecognized or ignored.

Psychological Disorders

Anxiety and depression are fundamental human experiences that may occur as normal emotional responses to stresses and life events but may develop into serious psychiatric disorders that can result in significant dysfunction. The term anxiety describes a state of worry or fear where a person anticipates danger or loss and is associated with many different types of psychiatric disorder. It frequently arises when a person feels his integrity, family, or job are threatened. Anxiety is one of the most common emotions that the population in general experiences with most of us experiencing occasional anxiety in response to the events of everyday living such as speaking in public or preparing for an interview. This anxiety is short lived and most people do not seek help from the medical community. The syndrome in its mildest form presents a person with a subjective feeling of dread. More severe reactions include a large variety of exaggerated responses involving mood, motor, cognition and physiological responses to the perceived dangers. The behavioral responses range from feelings of dread, decreased memory, poor concentration and apprehension to more disabling reactions such as phobias with avoidant behavior or obsessive compulsive rumination. The physiological symptoms are suggestive of autonomic arousal and include fast heart rate, shortness of breath or hyperventilation, sweating, chest pain, tremor, hyperactivity and difficulty swallowing. In addition, sleep difficulties, abdominal pain, nausea and diarrhea are common.

Anxiety usually develops early in life and becomes a pattern of response for the individual when stressed. The president most likely would be an individual that has been able to handle a great deal of pressure because of the level attained in his chosen career. However, anxiety can occur in anyone who becomes severely stressed and the president is certainly faced with many stresses because of the nature of his job. Certainly the president experiences some anxiety when facing the press, Congress, economic crisis, and military decisions.

A certain amount of anxiety can be helpful by helping a person attend to a particular problem or situation. This can help make for a satisfactory outcome. However, too much anxiety interferes with the person's ability to concentrate and often results in irritability, ambivalence, poor decision making and feelings of helplessness. These traits, if commonly experienced by the president, could greatly interfere with effectiveness of the office. Indecisiveness and ambivalence could cause the president to become an impotent leader thus weakening the presidency.

A severe form of anxiety known as a panic attack can result in which the individual feels as if he were dying and thus becomes paralyzed from fear. Phobic anxiety can develop in response to panic attacks thus making the person a prisoner to his own fear. In this case a president could begin to avoid press conferences, cabinet meetings and public engagements resulting in loss of leadership.

In addition, anxiety can be exogenously based and be caused by medications, withdrawal from medications, hyperthyroidism, angina, pheochromocytoma, Meniere's syndrome or asthma to name a few.

An additional problem may develop when the president attempts to control his anxiety with self medication using alcohol, tranquilizers or other drugs. These drugs may result in addiction, disorientation, confusion, sedation and impaired judgment, thus making the situation worse. Certainly all presidents have experienced anxiety but we may never know how the syndrome has affected the presidency and the course of the country.

Depression is also one of the most commonly experienced emotions. All human beings experience fluctuations in mood as a reaction to life events but this is not necessarily disabling. The word depression means many things to many people and encompasses the following range of clinical states: sadness, grief, chronic dysphoria to the full blown syndrome that we call major depression. We all experience depressed mood from time to time; however, the mood is short lived and does not darken our entire existence. These feelings resolve without medical intervention and generally do not result in significant social, economic or medical disability. In contrast, a major depressive episode often results in significant disability and may require medical intervention and hospitalization. Mild depression results from a maladaptive response to the disappointments and stress of daily living. The depression may be associated with the development of a chronic state of dysphoria or chronic sadness that causes mild impairment in relationships, occupational functioning and social activities. More pronounced states of depression are experienced by those individuals who develop dysthymic disorder. This illness generally begins at an early age and is life long with chronic feelings of depression interspersed with short periods of remissions. This psychiatric condition is associated with mild to moderate impairment in social and occupational functioning. It is possible that a president could have successfully attained the presidency despite this illness. However, chronic depression can interfere with judgment, energy levels, relationships and could potentially interfere with the effective leadership of the president. These depressions are not usually amenable to treatment with medications and would require psychotherapy or hospitalization.

A more severe depression can occur that is called major depressive episode. This is a common psychiatric illness with the first episode starting in the person's twenties or thirties but can occur at any age. Many people who experience one episode of major depression are likely to have recurrent episodes. The lifetime prevalence rate for the development of a major depression is approximately 15% in both men and women. The disorder most commonly involves depressed mood, decreased sleep, loss of interest in food, sex, and other pleasurable activities. Guilt, anhedonia or loss of pleasure, psychomotor retardation, feelings of worthlessness and self-reproach are common. In addition, recurrent thoughts of death, suicide or wishes to be dead are common. The cause of the illness is not exactly determined but is probably multifaceted involving genetic, environmental and chemical components.

This disease can result in significant distress with impairment in reasoning, decision making abilities, energy levels and concentration. In the most severe form psychosis develops as manifested by delusions, guilt, paranoia,

Norman J. Knorr, M.D. and Daniel Harrington, M.D.

hallucinations and impaired reality testing. Even moderately severe depressions can interfere with the effective functioning of the individual experiencing the depression. However, the more severe cases of depression may be life threatening because of the high risk of suicide. If a major depression were to develop in a president it is quite likely that significant dysfunction would occur resulting in impaired leadership and decision making abilities. This could result in delayed decisions, surrogate leadership, poorly based decisions and loss of leadership qualities.

Depression can be effectively treated using antidepressants, psychotherapy and Electroconvulsant Therapy (ECT). The issue over the ability to serve after successful treatment of a major depression was examined in 1972 when Thomas Eagleton was the Democratic vice presidential candidate. Shortly after the announcement of his nomination the public was informed that Senator Eagleton had experienced a major depression and had received ECT. With increasing public scrutiny, the Senator chose to withdraw from the race. Interestingly enough, since that time Senator Eagleton has received continued support from his constituency and continued until 1987 to serve in the Senate without obvious impairment in his abilities.

A severe problem could arise if the president developed a psychosis. Psychosis is a generic term that is associated with delusions, hallucinations, disorganized thinking, paranoia and irrational behavior resulting in loss of reality testing. Psychosis is the result of many disease processes ranging from many psychiatric disorders to structural and metabolic disorders that affect the brain. The main psychiatric disorders associated with psychosis are the following: mood disorders, schizophrenia, temporal lobe (brain) dysfunction, delusional disorders, reactions to severe stress, drug ingestion and drug withdrawal. The structural and metabolic disorders that may result in psychosis include: brain pathology (tumors, seizures, infections) and metabolic disorders, such as kidney failure, liver failure, hyperactive or hypoactive thyroid gland, electrolyte imbalances and low or high blood sugar.

Of the psychiatric disorders it would be unlikely for the president to develop psychosis from schizophrenia or mania because these disorders generally begin early in life and would declare themselves before age 35 which is the minimal age requirement for a person to be elected president. With schizophrenia a period of decline in functioning associated with poor self care, bizarre behavior, social isolation, as well as, hallucinations, delusions, and disorganization must be present for the diagnosis to be made. These signs and symptoms make it unlikely that the individual would be functional enough to achieve the status of a successful politician.

Psychosis associated with the manic state of a manic depressive illness could possibly develop for the first time in a person in the age range of thirty to forty but would be less likely to occur for the first time in those over the age of 45 to 50 years. Consequently, this type of psychosis is unlikely to affect the president but could be possible if the president were elected in his late thirties or early forties. Psychosis associated with mania may involve increased energy, loss of sleep, delusions of grandeur, rapid speech, impulsive behavior, impaired judgment, irritability and hallucinations. Many very successful politicians may suffer from the syndrome of hypomania that may involve increased energy, decreased need for sleep, gregariousness but without the severe impairment of a psychosis. In fact, these traits make that individual more productive as long as the psychotic level is not reached. Many successful lawyers, physicians and entertainment people have these qualities.

Under certain circumstances of severe stress psychosis may result in a clinical condition known as a brief reactive psychosis. This can occur in any person who is placed under unusually difficult circumstances and results in a brief period where hallucinations, delusions, paranoia and loss of reality occur. The premorbid functioning of the individual is good. The psychosis resolves after hours or days with return to a normal functional status. What could happen to the president and nation during this psychotic interim is too frightening to speculate upon.

Psychosis secondary to the use of medications or from the withdrawal from drugs is a common problem and could occur in a president. This is particularly true if addiction developed to a drug and abrupt discontinuation of the drug occurred. Drugs that may cause psychosis from their use or from withdrawal include the benzodiazepines, barbiturates,

114

alcohol, narcotic pain relievers as well as with a number of muscle relaxants such as baclofen. Idiosyncratic psychotic drug reactions can occur with commonly used drugs such as cimetidine and ranitidine (peptic ulcer medication), corticosteroids, digoxin and quinidine and procainamide (antiarrhythmic drugs). Idiosyncratic drug reactions and withdrawal are more likely to be seen with the older population which means the older president is more vulnerable to this problem.

Dementia

The aging brain has less capacity to withstand insults. Even in the elderly healthy person without evidence of significant brain disease small disturbances in equilibrium can result in various types of altered consciousness. The aging brain is more likely to experience confusion with jet lag, frequent change in surroundings, the addition of psychoactive medication or alcohol. In an elderly president where the business of the affairs of state requires him to travel, to keep late hours, to keep inconsistent schedules, and to imbibe in alcohol it is possible that the president might experience some confusion particularly at night when stimulation is minimal. This is known as sun downing and could result in impaired decision-making ability by the president if he were to experience this confusion during a critical moment.

Dementia is a devastating disease that has captured the interest of the public. With the population enjoying the benefits of improved health care, individuals are living to a longer life expectancy. As a result more of our elderly are suffering from the consequences of degenerative brain disease. Degenerative brain disease is a broad category that encompasses many illnesses that present with the final common pathway of dementia. The essential features of dementia include impairment in short and long term memory, associated with a decline in abstract reasoning, poor judgement, marked personality changes and other disturbances in higher brain functioning. The onset is generally insidious and is most commonly found in the elderly but may begin at any age.

The disorder is generally progressive except in the 15% of cases where a reversible cause is determined and appropriate treatment is begun. Recovery in these cases may be incomplete. The etiology of the degenerative brain diseases is varied with the most common cause being Alzheimer's Disease followed by multi-infarct dementia (vascular disease), brain infections, syphilis, tuberculosis, viral and fungal meningitis, Acquired Immune Deficiency Syndrome (AIDS), brain trauma, toxic metabolic causes (pernicious anemia, folate deficiency, hypothyroidism), normal pressure hydrocephalus, Huntington's chorea, multiple sclerosis and Parkinson's Disease.

Certainly there have been two presidents where cognitive difficulties were noticed during their years as president. President Wilson suffered from a stroke while in office and experienced cognitive impairment, speech difficulties, irritability and depression. President Roosevelt died three months into his fourth term of office. During the last year of Roosevelt's life he suffered from heart failure and showed signs of chronic fatigue, recurrent respiratory infections and transient head and chest pain. It was during this time that Mr. Roosevelt participated in the Yalta Conference to settle post World War II European peace. Historians state that his health was so poor and his stamina and mental abilities so impaired that his health was a liability that resulted in a Soviet advantage in post World War II division of Europe. These two episodes are examples where probable degenerative brain disease significantly interfered with the president's discharge of his duties.

Personality Disorder

The personality traits of the president certainly influence the manner in which he deals with stress, manages people and handles conflict. Personality refers to a set of relatively stable and predictable habits that characterize the way a person manages day to day living. It functions to stabilize relationships, protecting the individual from traumatic surprises and overt psychological symptom formation. In its action as a protective armor it is rigid and protects but at the same time limits freedom of thought and action. This rigidity tends to increase in the face of

116

threats, thus decreasing the repertoire of behaviors the individual has at his disposal. All human beings use this mechanism for protection and for most of us it serves us well. However, certain individuals when stressed may have an exacerbation of their personality traits resulting in the development of a personality disorder or other psychiatric illness that can be more disabling and destructive than the personality trait.

For example, an individual who by nature is suspicious of others and of certain situations can under severe conditions (illness, marital stress, drugs) develop a more serious and dangerous condition that results in paranoia. This paranoia causes the person to feel that others are out to harm him and thus suspiciousness and mistrust of others develops. The paranoid person cannot own up to the responsibility for these feelings and places the problem on others. This results in distrust of others and inability to share with others. In addition the paranoid person may take a defensive action based on the suspicious belief that others will harm him.

The stresses of the presidency probably bring out the best and the worst traits in the individual charged with the duty of leading the country. All of us have personality traits which influence the way in which we form relationships, handle stress, cope with defeat and make decisions. These traits help us develop into the person that we are. It is when the traits become more predictable and the person's actions become more programmed that problems develop. Personality traits are what helps a person appeal to the public to attain the office of president but can also be his undoing when placed under stresses of leadership, illness or loss.

Anesthesia

Another situation that has occurred that results in the temporary inability of the president to discharge his duties is when the president undergoes local or general anesthesia. In both of these instances mind altering medications are given to do either local or general surgery so that the person undergoing the surgery does not experience pain and discomfort. This is particularly true during general anesthesia where a person is put to sleep during the surgery and may require many hours to days to recover. In this case the president would be unable to perform his duties during surgery as well as for an unspecified time after surgery. In addition, pain medications which have significant nervous system effects are generally given postoperatively. This could interfere with judgement, mood and the level of consciousness. During the surgery itself the 25th Amendment provides for the elective transfer of power to the vice president until the president is capable of discharging his duties. A dilemma arises post-operatively as to when the president is capable of taking over the reins of power. In fact, this issue was raised in the case of President Reagan following the removal of malignant polyps of the colon. Following the surgery for colon cancer on July 13, 1985 speculation has been raised that President Reagan may have discussed shipment of arms to Iran in the recovery period during which he may have been under the influence of drugs. This raises issues about the use of the 25th Amendment and the need for uniform periods of disability after surgery and the need for physician involvement in making the determination of ability to resume duties.

Discussion

Psychological disability exists when an individual, because of impaired mental health, becomes incapable of carrying out his or her normal day to day activities. To impose upon the disabled person the obligation of maintaining the responsibilities of his or her work only exacerbates the problem. The sufferer of the psychological distress becomes more sick and the work situation disorganized and chaotic.

In the case of a disabled president, the people working with him, staff and family alike, would tend to deny the onset of psychological problems and the deleterious impact it would exert on the functioning of the office. Early in the illness, hope would exist the president will "snap out of it." As the disability continues, the tendency is for the spouse and White House staff to assume the responsibilities, wherever possible, of the chief executive and to "cover up" his dysfunction. The president's disability and the surrogating of power continues while the office becomes more disorganized, decision and policy makers cannot be accurately identified, and the president becomes less visible. The denial of illness is always more intense when dealing with psychological illness as compared to the physical and the "cover up" may extend over a long period of time. The 25th Amendment is not considered because of the expectation that tomorrow will be better. In addition, great reluctance will exist as the family and staff will equate their disclosing the president's disability as being disloyal. It is unlikely the president will invoke the 25th Amendment as persons with psychological disorder from whatever origin often lack the insight to self determine their level of disability. Other politicians will avoid responsibility since they instinctively understand the consequences of becoming the "messenger" of bad news. The president's cabinet and staff fear their jobs are in jeopardy if the 25th Amendment is invoked and the chief executive cannot return to work quickly. Who then will disclose the president's plight? The stresses of a psychological disorder are always felt most keenly by the family. Hopefully the spouse will step forward and verbalize the need for help. Unfortunately this has not occurred in the past when former presidents were disabled with severe debilitating illness. Nor did any of the other persons mentioned above disclose the president's disability.

If the spouse, or others, acknowledge the need for medical assistance for the president's psychological disorder, it would be described in terms of the need for treatment of a physical illness. The president's problems would not be disclosed as psychological, or even nervous, but rather as fatigue, difficult recovery from the flu, etc. Whatever the circumstances of disclosure of the president's illness, and however the 25th Amendment is invoked, the important considerations are that a human being will receive the help they require to get well, and order will finally return to government. Hopefully the above will be accomplished before the media discloses the president's disability and public confidence in the government erodes.

The president's personal physician has purposely been neglected, thus far in this paper, as a participant in the

119

25th Amendment process. Many health professionals would concur that a physician is bound by oath to maintain patient confidentiality and disclosing the state of the president's health to others, for any reason, is a violation of that oath. An ethical predicament becomes obvious when physical or psychological disability is an issue. For the physician to remain silent, in defense of his oath, and allow a disabled person to remain on the job with deteriorating health problems is not providing appropriate medical treatment. In fact, the first step in the treatment of someone with psychological disorder is to remove them from the stressful environment that has initiated or aggravated their illness.

The president's physician is not mentioned in the 25th Amendment. Perhaps the physician's job description needs a review. Instead of identifying the physician as personal, should the physician's role in supplying medical care at the White House be more consistent with those who work in industry? Company doctors have responsibilities to their employers and they are expected to report certain patient information to the employer. They must certainly report on an employee who is disabled and incapable of working. This model has some basis in fact since the employer of the president's physician is the American taxpayer. Using the industry model would establish the physician's right to disclose to the vice president, with the aid of expert consultant reports, the disability of the president if the president ignored or refused the physician's request to consider invoking the 25th Amendment.

As an adjunct to the appointment of the president's physician, a Mental Health consultant appointed to assist the White House physician could present opportunities for the president, the first family, and staff to seek advice and counsel regarding psychological matters. The stresses of Watergate and the Iran/Contra episode on the president and his staff, and the existence of alcoholism among the president's family and staff is good evidence that such a service is needed. Unfortunately the stigmata of psychological disorder still exists in some quarters and such an appointment would be viewed as undesirable by persons with political career ambitions.

The 25th Amendment to the Constitution of the United States of America was adopted in 1966 to help avert possible difficulties that could be encountered when a situation arose where a president was unable to carry out his responsibilities. The amendment provides for the removal of the president from his responsibilities if unable to fulfill his job because of medical disability. There has been infrequent use of the 25th Amendment since its adoption in 1966, except in the rare instances where the president was unexpectedly placed in the position that he was unable to carry out the responsibilities as the president of the United States. A recent event was the attempted assassination of President Reagan in 1981. In this episode it was clear that the President was unable to carry out his required tasks. The amendment has several sections that provide for the smooth transition of power to the appropriate leader, usually the vice president. Section 3 provides for the elective transfer of power when circumstances arise that the president knows will make him unable to maintain power, such as during general anesthesia associated with general surgery. Section 4 has been included for those unusual circumstances when concern has been raised about the president's competency to conduct the normal affairs of state. Section 4 has never been used to remove the president from office. Although passed by the Congress to provide for the smooth transition in cases of incompetence secondary to medical problems, it is unclear as to how smoothly the transfer of power would be if the 25th Amendment were invoked.

PRESIDENTIAL ILLNESS

James F. Childress

NARRATOR: Today we have the very special privilege of having our colleague and friend Jim Childress here who, but for one reason would have been on our Presidential Disability Commission. That reason is that he has, to the joy of us all, picked the wrong university. As some of you know we've avoided asking local people to serve on commissions but rather use them in the capacity of staff. We planned to have a full session in Washington with Jim Childress but it is every bit as good to have a discussion in this setting.

Not very many years ago, and I say this not in condescension but in envy, Jim Childress was born in Mount Airy, North Carolina. He early established himself in two fields. At Guilford College he had not only an excellent academic record but the highest kick as a baseball pitcher in the history of that school! He received a BD, MA and Ph.D. from the Yale Graduate School. He became an assistant professor in the Department of Religious Studies in 1968 at Virginia at the age of 28 and in 1972 was named Chairman of the Department of Religious Studies. Much to the sorrow of everyone here, Georgetown lured him away with the Joseph Kennedy Sr. Distinguished Professorship in Christian Ethics but fortunately in 1981 he came to his senses and returned to the University of Virginia, much to our benefit.

His best known works are writings on civil disobedience and political obligation, on moral responsibility and nonviolence and on violence and war. In the subject that he will discuss today, he has written such books as *Priorities in Biomedical Ethics, Who should Decide: Paternalism in Health Care* and a co-authored book,

123

Principles of Biomedical Ethics. He has several other books forthcoming. On the specific topic of confidentiality (for those of you who want to read further) he has written "Medical Confidentiality: Who Protects the Victims?" *Pharos* Vol. 40; "Citizen and Physician: Harmonious or Conflicting Responsibilities", *The Journal of Medicine and Philosophy*, Vol. 2; and he has co-authored an article for *Theoretical Medicine* on "Metaphors and Models of Doctor-Patient Relationships." He has served as vice chairman of the federal Task Force on Organ Transplantation, and he is a member of the Subcommittee on Human Gene Therapy and the Data and Safety Monitoring Board for AIDS Drug Trials. He is, in other words, one of the nation's most distinguished observers in the interface between science, technology, law and ethics. So we count ourselves privileged to have an opportunity to hear and then talk with Jim Childress this morning on confidentiality in doctor-patient relationships.

MR. CHILDRESS: Thanks very much Ken for that glowing but unmerited introduction which I will nevertheless accept. In thinking about our topic today, I recalled the story that Premier Nikita Khrushchev reportedly told President Kennedy. According to the story, a man was arrested for shouting in the Kremlin: "Khrushchev is a fool! Khrushchev is a fool!" He was tried, convicted and then sentenced to twenty-five years of hard labor in Siberia: five years for defaming the Premier, and twenty years for revealing a state secret.

Unfortunately, our topic is not so humorous, largely because of the specter of risk that our country and the world at large would face from an ill president—particularly if the president is so ill, mentally or physically, that he could not effectively exercise the duties of office but nonetheless continues in that role. The biggest fear, perhaps, is a nuclear confrontation.

The following description of *Presidential Courage* by Dr. John Moses and Wilbur Cross appeared in an announcement of the book:

> Although many of our chief executives have been plagued by debilitating illness, the one enduring quality they share is courage. This book shows

124

how they overcame enormous physical and mental handicaps to discharge their heavy official duties.

The general question behind our discussion may be stated as "when does presidential courage become foolhardiness, putting large numbers of people at tremendous risk?" Courage is usually a virtue but sometimes it may be a vice.

It is easy to focus on the moral dilemmas that might emerge for the president's physician (and for others) who try to balance their loyalties to the president and their loyalties to the country and to the world. I will return to those dilemmas from the standpoint of the ethics of confidential relations, but one major ethical responsibility is to prevent such dilemmas. There will always be uncertainty, but dilemmas can be reduced by clearly indicating the lines of responsibility. Appropriate rules and procedures can reduce the dilemmas that any one person or group of persons would face. Nonetheless, discharging this ethical responsibility to reduce dilemmas will not be easy because we want to avoid two sorts of incentives: We don't want to make it too easy or too hard to remove the president for mental or physical disability. We seek such a balance because decisions of this kind might be very consequential for the country and the world. This balance is a very practical matter which ethical theory may not illuminate very clearly.

I'm going to sketch the rule or rules of confidentiality as they have developed to govern relationships between physicians and patients. We shall try to see why those rules are so widespread, why they are so important, and what kinds of limits in both range and strength have been recognized. Then we shall examine how general considerations about the doctor-patient relationship and rules of confidentiality in that relationship might illuminate the relationship between the president and his physician. We will also consider whether current rules of confidentiality are adequate to deal with the problem we are examining today.

Let me begin with the general ethical problem of confidentiality in the doctor-patient relationship. The essence of the rule of confidentiality is the right of patients to control further access to personal information in their relationship with physicians and other health care professionals. To put it another way: the physician or other health care professional has a duty to respect a patient's right to confidentiality. At the very least, a rule of confidentiality must prohibit *some* disclosures or *some* information by physicians and other health care professionals to *some* third parties without the consent of the patient. Otherwise we would not have a rule of confidentiality. Basically, when the patient enters into a relationship with the physician, the patient grants the doctor access to himself or herself in order to gain the benefits of that relationship. These benefits include diagnostic, prognostic and therapeutic procedures. And the rule of confidentiality prohibits the physician from disclosing information about the patient to third parties, unless the patient authorizes the disclosure.

Now let me just say a word about privacy in relation to confidentiality. In entering a relationship with a health care professional the patient obviously surrenders some of his or her privacy, for example, by allowing the professional to touch him or her or by disclosing personal information. We always lose privacy when we enter into such relationships but we are willing to yield privacy in order to gain important benefits. The information that emerges in those relationships is protected by confidentiality. If a third party breaks into a doctor's office and gains access to the files, the third party violates the rule of privacy, rather than the rule of confidentiality. Only the physician or other health care professional can violate the rule of confidentiality by disclosing information to others without the patient's permission.

Rules of confidentiality appear in practically all societies. Examples include the Hippocratic oath, which states, "What I may see or hear about my patient's life in the course of treatment, I shall on no account spread abroad, holding such things shameful to be spoken about." Likewise the AMA Principles of Medical Ethics in the 1980s affirm that a physician "shall safeguard patient confidences within the constraints of law." Many more examples from other cultures could be given.

Why are rules of confidentiality so widespread? In part because they are considered useful and in part because

maxim or rule of thumb, such as "Don't bunt on the third strike." In my view it has substantial weight and is binding, other things being equal. When the physician believes that it should be breached, he or she has to bear the burden of proof and show that under the circumstances there are good reasons for doing so.

In the Tarasoff case, if the courts had not held that a client's threat to kill someone else is not be protected under rules of confidentiality, then a physician would have to decide whether he or she should disclose that information in order to protect any potential victims. In recent years the question has been raised whether physicians should warn spouses or lovers of patients with AIDS, especially if the patient has not told his or her lover or spouse and is not practicing safe sex. This is currently the most controversial topic in the discussion of the rule of confidentiality. How does a physician balance the duty of confidentiality with the duty to protect third parties who may be put at risk by the patient's actions?

I think that several conditions need to be met before a physician or another health care professional can justifiably breach the rule of confidentiality. One condition is that other people must be at serious risk. "Risk" refers to both the probability of some harm occurring and to the magnitude of that harm. The following chart indicates possible variations in risk:

RISK ANALYSIS

		Magnitude of Harm	
		Minor	Major
Probability of	Low	1	2
Harm's Occurrence	High	3	4

So how should we deal with possible and probable harms in deciding whether to breach confidentiality? If there is a low probability of a minor harm occurring, or even a high probability of a minor harm occurring, it is not justifiable to breach confidentiality. If there is a high probability of major harm to another party we come the closest to satisfying the first condition for justified disclosure. If there is only a low probability of a major harm, matters are more complicated. Perhaps there is only a one in a thousand chance that a mentally or physically impaired president would initiate an action leading to a nuclear holocaust, but this is a very, very serious harm to humanity. So, in deciding whether to disclose we're really trying to determine whether there is a high probability of serious harm or, to a certain extent, a low probability of a serious harm.

The second condition is that the disclosure must be suited to avoid the serious harm, and that the benefits of disclosure must outweigh its harms. Of course, there will often be harms in disclosure—not only to the person in question but perhaps also to others—and there possible or probable harms must be balanced against and outweighted by the probable benefits.

A third condition is that that there must be no morally satisfactory alternatives. It may well be, for example, that the professional could persuade the patient to reveal the information himself or herself.

Finally, the disclosure should be as limited as possible in the circumstances. That is, it should include only the amount and kind of information required to prevent the harm.

How might we proceed to think about the physician's role in relation to the president? One possibility is to require candidates for the office of president (and perhaps for some other high offices) to disclose more about their health in the first place and to authorize their physicians to do likewise. Such candidates would be obligated to instruct their physicians to disclose the relevant information. While there would be a considerable loss of privacy, it would be yielded in the interest of the country. And it may be appropriate to reduce privacy in order to avoid violating confidentiality. The privacy debate raging in the aftermath of the Gary Hart affair is about the limits of public interest in contrast to public curiosity. Curiosity has its limits, and need not be pandered to. Public interest is less limited, and it certainly extends to the president's health.

Yet we have to be careful about imposing a duty on the physician inconsistent with the president's wishes. If we make the duty to disclose too strong then we run the risk that the president will not seek help when needed and possibly create a worse situation. It is important to balance both benefits and harms in formulating the rule. One possibility would be to require the president to undergo periodic mental and physical examinations as part of office-holding. Such examinations could be conducted by impartial physicians, perhaps constituting or advising a health monitoring board. Because the decision to breach confidentiality would be a difficult burden for any individual to bear, we need to devise public mechanisms to determine the president's health and remove him when appropriate. In short, we need a policy to reduce the burden on the president's physician and to place it on a public body. A public procedure would not entail broadcasting the information, but it must contain an assurance of the president's accountability to the public. Prospective rather than retrospective accountability should be our aim.

However, such a mechanism may not provide for a situation in which the president tells his physician not to disclose to the Congress, or to the public, information concerning his ill health, which the physician believes impairs the president's ability to govern. It may be difficult to specify the scope of the rule of confidentiality in advance to deal with the president's physician. I imagine that it will have to be somewhat vague. In the case where the president does not consent to disclosure, the physician will have to balance his or her duty to the president against his or her duty to the country and the world. How might the physician balance these duties? As I have argued, confidentiality is so important, even in this setting, that any breach requires sound reasons. The physician must believe that the country is at serious risk, that disclosure would probably protect the country, that the benefits of disclosure would outweigh other costs flowing from it, and that there are no morally acceptable alternatives. In

131

addition, the physician must strive to limit the scope of disclosure to protect confidentiality as much as possible while still protecting the country. The issue of who should be told is difficult to settle too: Should the public be notified or just certain leaders?

In the presidential case the physician has to be worried about any physical or mental impairments that would then lead to conduct that would put others at risk. The four conditions identified presuppose that the physician has made a defensible judgment that the physical or mental impairments are such that they really do put others at risk, for instance, by creating potential political, military or other problems.

I am proposing a strict ethical position, which asks whether there is any other way the physician could reduce the potential risk to the country (and the world) without breaching confidentiality. The best way would be to persuade the president to disclose some information himself. If the physician is unable to do so, then he or she faces some tough decisions.

QUESTION: I was thinking of the President not being able to remember the name of the United Nations Security Council at his press conference. One could say this suggests that something isn't working up there. But you could also say that somebody had been talking constantly about arms control and that the President was on top of that issue. The White House people might argue that. Also, this administration has not been noted for its use of the UN. Maybe Reagan has forgotten about it too. Once I briefed Archibald Cary when he became deputy UN ambassador in the Eisenhower administration. His first question was, "Where is it?" So there are all kinds of things. With AIDS patients you *can* say that certain behavior involves risk to others, can't you?

MR. CHILDRESS: Your question seems to be whether behavior of an ill person is deliberate or not, and in fact the outcome of his disease. Let's suppose that an AIDS patient is putting sexual partners at risk by not disclosing his infection and not practicing safe sex. Here the physician's task is less a medical assessment about the

132

patient's mental fitness than moral judgment to intervene in the patient's life and warn the patient's partners about the risks. In the case of the president the physician would primarily have to make a medical assessment as to the severity of any mental or physical impairment.

QUESTION: I wonder if you can deal with a scenario which seems to have occurred. The president has been seriously disabled but he has a superb wife who can sign his name incredibly well and because of that the risk assessment is in the low category. Now the fact is he can't preside worth a damn and the doctor is aware of it. What would you do with him?

MR. CHILDRESS: You still may have a sense that certain actions are not being taken to protect the national interest, even with the president's wife being able to sign important directives. The president's spouse may not be able to handle a nuclear confrontation. That risk is still there and that's what you are evaluating. But note that these judgments hinge in effect on an assessment of what *she* is able to do and not simply an assessment of what he is unable to do.

COMMENT: What I am suggesting is that, at all given points, we have morally acceptable alternatives, whether it's the vice president, the Cabinet, or the spouse. If we want to hide the disability of the president, we have mechanisms for doing it and carrying on the work of the country. I think this is improper. Another question is whether the doctor should be involved in that decision-making at all or be limited to judging the ability of the president to function, and whether at that second stage, the decision-making should be taken over by the commission you were referring to or in some other fashion.

MR. CHILDRESS: I'm talking about the justified breach of confidentiality. In part of your scenario people are respecting confidentiality. What I want to suggest is that disclosing personal medical information without the patient's consent to anyone is a breach of confidentiality. So when you say we have other people we can go to, that too would involve a breach of confidentiality.

COMMENT: After concluding that he is seriously disabled would that be appropriate?

MR. CHILDRESS: There are different degrees of mental disability and you are right that we have a procedure for dealing with such a disability. However, I'm talking about a case in which the president refuses to disclose information about a disability that the professional has good reason to believe could cause serious harm. There are ways to deal with that situation as well. Setting up rules and procedures that would guarantee the kind of disclosure we think is appropriate would be one way. We don't have to put the burden on the physician. We can put the burden on the candidate or even set up a public board that would monitor the president's health. I'd be in favor of setting up public mechanisms and put the physician mainly in a consultative role. There would be no breach of confidentiality because a president would expect to be monitored by a public board.

QUESTION: Jim, you have a unique capacity to answer potential questions. You have already answered many of mine. I would like to carry on this discussion in a somewhat different way and focus not on the possible irrationality of a president, but on the rationality of those around him and those who conduct the affairs of government. There is very little that a president can personally do to damage anything. If a president, for example, makes an irrational demand on Congress, Congress will simply ignore him. But what about his administration? In the last twenty years presidents have surrounded themselves with people who are utterly devoted to them, both personally as well as politically. That is not to imply that these people can't remain rational. I understand that Hitler in the last days of World War II ordered the destruction of Paris, a highly irrational and immoral order. His officers simply ignored it and refused to carry it out. I'm suggesting that if the president gets out of hand, people will react and proceed to put barriers in the way of irrational orders. I see a great deal of resilience in government that, at least to some degree, modifies the problems with which we are dealing.

COMMENT: Some people working in the Nixon presidency said they came to realize that when Nixon would say, "You ought to bomb Brookings," or "You ought to take away all the grants that were to be awarded to MIT," he didn't mean it because three days later he would say to them, "You haven't taken any money from MIT have you?" That's illustrative of this point.

MR. CHILDRESS: I did not mean to underestimate the significance of both formal and informal processes in the White House for protecting the nation's interest. But you're thinking about irrationality in terms of means to an end. Irrational ends themselves are something else. Nor is all irrationality necessarily rooted in some mental or physical impairment. I guess one of the concerns I would still have is whether we have some mechanism for making sure the public interest is served.

COMMENT: Preconditions for being the president's physician have to be very explicit or I wouldn't take the job. One should understand what goes on between the President and the people around him before he takes on that job. I think that's enough.

COMMENT: Where the medical man gets confused is when he has to make some non-technical judgment on the behavior of the president as relates to his personal and public life. We are all confused about that at the moment. A physician going into this role has to make up his mind beforehand about what he is going to do. Conditions should be clear before taking on this job.

MR. CHILDRESS: If I heard you correctly you were suggesting that the physician attending the president should make sure that, even if there were the kind of public mechanisms we discussed, he would not have to disclose certain information.

COMMENT: As a physician I know that in order for the patient to trust me and for me to be able to help my patient significantly, I need some of this kind of leeway. Therefore I would not be willing to abandon my own judgment in balancing my obligations to the patient and to the country.

MR. CHILDRESS: Let me just ask you one question on the obligation of assuming that role. Would you do it? How would you handle confidentiality if you were the president's physician? Let's say there were no rules as to what we are talking about with the President.

COMMENT: I would talk with him about what he wants to talk about and then I would negotiate with him on the kinds of things he wouldn't want me to say. I would hope he would say, "Go ahead and tell them everything. I'm sacrificing my privacy." If he did not, as Churchill did not with Lord Moran, I would feel I had to make some political judgment as to disclosure.

COMMENT: I'd like to ask something about this system which political scientists should know. Presidents can fire every subordinate *à la* Lansing and Wilson. He can fire his physician as well. He can fire anybody that doesn't agree with him. It seems to me that if he is crazy and fires everybody, he still has power. If you are firing everybody in sight you are alerting the whole country that there is something wrong. There will still be barriers of one kind of another and the farther you go in that direction, the more you are telling everybody that there is irrationality at the top.

QUESTION: You have raised very interesting questions and in doing so there has been very frequent use of the word "rule." I wonder if you would discuss in what context you use that word. Is it a broad one, as a substitute for a statute, a custom or a desirable course of events? Does it represent hopes, aspirations, or something else?

MR. CHILDRESS: When I talk about a "rule" or "rules" of confidentiality, I simply use those terms as shorthand

James F. Childress

expressions to focus on either the patient's right or the physician's obligation to do certain things regarding further access to the information. I'm really talking about the rule(s) of confidentiality in the context of the tradition of medical ethics. It happens also to be a rule our society has recognized, as most other societies have, as very important, and our society also has laws to protect confidentiality within limits.

QUESTION: From what I see and hear, we have no trouble with determining the president's or almost anybody else's physical condition. As a matter of fact, they normally give you all the details of the operations telling you the president's physical disability poses no threat except where it affects his mental or emotional state. With FDR, I remember there were a lot of people who thought that his paralysis affected his mind, particularly those who were against him. Leaving those things aside, you are concerned with the mental and emotional normality—if you want to call it that—and here you get into what seems to be the heart of the problem. But there is no attempt to regulate or decide whether the President is mentally healthy or not. It depends on the competency of the people who are judging his competence, and you alluded to that.

Another thing is that we are getting away from realism. Normal people, sometimes do very silly things; all of us do. You can't make angels out of us, and I think you have to be very careful to give someone the power to judge a powerful man. It just doesn't make any sense, and I think we should ease off. As Mr. Graebner suggests, there appears to be enough natural checks so presidents don't get too badly out of hand. Physicians are skillful and well trained but they don't always have very broad minds. They haven't had time to develop them! To have them judge the mental and emotional capacity of a president is not proper.

MR. CHILDRESS: I think that's a very important point.

COMMENT: Any physician judging on this will admit that psychiatrists are probably more familiar with these problems than the physician likely to attend the president. Our track record of predicting mental problems is not very good and the problem of deciding what is a "serious risk" worries me. I am thinking of the Eagleton situation where there was a previous depression dealt with under an assumed name nobody knew. How do I as the president's physician decide how serious this risk is? How much chance is there of his developing another depression, or becoming suicidal and risking war because of some paranoia like Secretary Forrestal had? That's a very tough decision and, I suggest, influenced by the physician's political orientation. If he's a Democrat then even an impaired Democrat is better than a Republican. His judgments are not going to be objective.

NARRATOR: Wouldn't you say that you were trying to deal with that kind of thing, though, in your risk analysis?

MR. CHILDRESS: In terms of predicting dangerousness, you are quite right that the track record is not good; it is difficult to predict dangerousness. This goes back to one of your earlier questions on predicting conduct. Yet it does seem to me that if we are in a situation where there is a very *low probability* of a *serious harm* being done, even if we think there may be some problems, the conditions are not present to justify a breach of confidentiality. I guess what I've said about the conditions that justify a breach of confidentiality could be interpreted much more broadly than I intended. But in fact very few circumstances would qualify.

What I think is more important comes out of your suggestions concerning the mechanisms and procedures to deal with president's health problems short of breaching confidentiality. Perhaps we need to revise our mechanisms along the lines you suggest.

QUESTION: I think there's an absolute necessity to make judgments. We've had two occasions of disability with Mr. Reagan where his staff had absolutely no idea of what happens to a person who has just had a major operation and anesthesia. On both occasions his staff "gave him the office back" at a time when, in my opinion and the opinion of 99 percent of the doctors, he was incompetent to take it back. The classical case was following his cancer surgery. You don't give the president back his office twelve hours after he has had his guts out. And we may find out during the Iran-Contra hearings that the president told Poindexter to go ahead in Iran some twenty-two hours after his cancer surgery. In these instances I think medical opinion is exceedingly important. Now Mr. Brownell and Mr. Bayh taught me that this doesn't happen very often, and I thoroughly agreed. But every once in a while a medical analysis has to be used by the staff.

NARRATOR: Jim Childress, thank you very much.

CONCLUDING OBSERVATIONS

Illness and disability are facts of life for most Americans yet presidents apparently are considered immune from illnesses and diseases that prevent them from performing their duties. If this were not so, why should constitutional provision for disability have been delayed until the late 1960s? Even then, why have presidents, and in particular President Reagan, been reluctant to acknowledge the invoking of the amendment? What are the social and psychological factors that account for this reluctance?

The authors of major essays in this little volume have addressed such questions. Beyond that, they have examined particular forms of disability to which presidents, like all the rest of us are subject. Senator Bayh in the opening essay has explored the new constitutional instrument for dealing with presidential disability and Professor Childress, in the concluding paper, has studied the dual responsibility of the presidential physicians to their patient and to the national interest.

Throughout, the discussion of presidential disability focuses essentially on two basic issues. They are, first, what can be said, more or less authoritatively, about specific physical, mental and emotional illnesses, and, second, what conclusions can be drawn from what is known about various illnesses and disabilities in relation to the new mechanism of the Twenty-fifth Amendment for safeguarding the American political system against presidential disability?

If one conclusion stands out in the present volume it is the authors' unanimity that the Twenty-fifth does provide a rational and orderly method for protecting the republic against the worst case scenario of presidential disability. No one would claim that the amendment's procedures are self-executing or that the personal wishes of a president may not influence its use. What is clear, however, is the availability of a single constitutional channel for the transfer and recovery of the powers and duties of the presidency. Also it appears that the availability of certain well-defined constitutional provisions supersede earlier stopgap arrangements such as written agreements between presidents and vice presidents.

This being true, the important question is whether a president will or will not make use of the amendment. The authors and the Miller Center Commission on presidential disability explored this question in some depth. The Commission in particular (see Annex A) found unconvincing the president's claim that he should not formally invoke the amendment for fear of establishing a precedent for his successor. The authors of the papers and Commission members were also highly skeptical of the argument that a president might cause a stock market crisis or alarm the international community through its use. Instead, authorities such as Senator Bayh and Attorney General Brownell maintain that the use of the amendment by successive presidents will lead to increasing confidence in its case. When the people see that presidential disability is provided for through a well-formulated constitutional amendment, they will be reassured. Once presidents come to take the amendment for granted, they will use it when necessary thus demonstrating that the Constitution provides for yet another eventuality in the process of governance.

This brings us to a central purpose of the volume and the Commission report. One of the unfulfilled needs which underlies presidential invoking of the twenty-fifth amendment is education. If cabinet members were ignorant of the provisions of the amendment, as was apparently the case at the time of the Reagan assassination attempt (see Fielding testimony, pp. 164-68), the public at large could hardly be better informed. The Miller Center Commission and the contributors to this volume believe that an educational campaign must be launched to remedy this deficiency. We call on the three national groups represented on the Commission to join in such an endeavor. We hope that other organizations with large and important constituencies in the public at large will join in the dissemination of information about the amendment. We make this appeal believing that if the public had a deeper understanding of the amendment as such and the machinery for the transfer of presidential powers and duties which it provides, their knowledge and confidence would feed back on the president. It might therefore relieve concern that its use would cause public alarm and a sense of crisis in the nation and the world.

In organizing the Commission and the preparation of this volume, the Miller Center intends to contribute to public education and, through such education, improvement of self-government in the American republic.

ANNEX A

Report of
The Miller Center Commission
On Presidential Disability
And the Twenty-fifth Amendment

WHITE BURKETT MILLER CENTER OF PUBLIC AFFAIRS

AT THE UNIVERSITY OF VIRGINIA

Table of Contents

The Miller Center Commission on Presidential Disability and the 25th Amendment is the fourth national commission established by the Center. The first of the commissions dealt with the conduct of presidential press conferences. Press secretary James Brady, in introducing President Reagan's first press conference, held up the commission's report and announced that the President intended to follow its recommendations. Governor Linwood Holton and former NBC White House correspondent Ray Scherer chaired that commission.

The second commission reviewed the state of the presidential nominating process and was chaired by former secretary of defense Melvin Laird and former U.S. Senator from Illinois Adlai Stevenson III. Its members numbering approximately fifty respected past and present political leaders included the current incumbent chairmen of the two major political parties and their immediate predecessors. The report's recommendations overlapped at certain points with the recommendations of the Hunt Commission; the two commissions had some modest influence on national party decisions, especially by the Democratic National Committee. (For example, the DNC decided to increase the number of elected officials at national conventions and urged a narrowing of the time frame for primaries and party caucuses.) One member predicted that the commission's focus on perennial problems in the process assured it would have "a long afterlife."

The third Miller Center commission co-chaired by two former secretaries of state, William P. Rogers and Cyrus R. Vance, analyzed presidential transitions and foreign policy. Its membership included three past secretaries of state and three former secretaries of defense as well as key participants on both sides of each postwar presidential transition beginning with the transition from Truman to Eisenhower. The commission's mandate foreshadowed some of the issues with which the fourth commission on presidential disability has grappled and their work overlapped at points.

The history of the fourth commission reflects a convergence of factors that made its creation possible.

First, the two principal authors of the 25th Amendment, former Eisenhower attorney general Herbert Brownell and former U.S. senator from Indiana Birch Bayh, accepted invitations to serve as co-chairmen. Second, the leaders of important national organizations such as the League of Women Voters, the American Bar Association and the American Medical Association were available to participate and to assist in the dissemination of the report to concerned bodies of the citizenry. Third, respected former congressmen, senators, a former presidential counsel and the recently retired chief justice joined the group. Fourth, staff at the University of Virginia, most notably Dr. Kenneth Crispell, former vice president for Health Affairs at the University of Virginia, had done significant research on presidential illness. Fifth, the W. Alton Jones Foundation provided generous funding to enable the Miller Center to proceed with the project. Taken together these five factors made possible the launching of the commission and the successful conduct of its meetings which have been held largely in Washington, D.C.

Since 1985, the Commission has held some half dozen working sessions. Staff work has been carried on at the Miller Center. Professor Paul Stephan of the University of Virginia Law School has played a leading role in the legal research required by the Commission and his colleague Professor Daniel Meador has offered helpful suggestions. Six excellent presentations at the Miller Center by Crispell, Dr. Knight Aldrich, Dr. Norman Knorr, Professor James Childress, Dr. Leonard Emmerglick and Professor Paul Stephan supplement the work of the Commission and will be published in a forthcoming volume of working papers.

The main draftsman of the report is Mr. Chalmers M. Roberts, former political and diplomatic reporter for the *Washington Post*. His mastery of the subject matter and of clear and concise literary expression have resulted, in his words, in "turning legalese into journalese." The Commission is most grateful for his dedicated and informed research and writing through the summer of 1987 and respectfully dedicates the report to him. I should acknowledge the appreciation expressed by the Commission to the Miller Center and myself for organizing and coordinating this effort. I would in turn thank them for their dedication, informed judgment and unquestioned intelligence on complex medical and political issues.

152

Five staff members deserve special mention. Mrs. Anne Hobbs typed the original transcripts of all Commission meetings. Mrs. Pat Dunn edited and made corrections in all Commission meeting transcripts and papers for volume of special presentations. Ms. Shirley Kohut prepared the papers for the volume of special presentations and typed and made corrections in various versions of the final report. She has been tireless in assisting in the work of four national commissions. Mr. Reed Davis attended every working session but one and was responsible for the efficient conduct of commission meetings. Mr. Peter Tester attended the final session and joined in the editing of the report. Finally, Ms. Nancy Lawson helped when supplementary typing and editing were most needed.

Kenneth W. Thompson, Director
White Burkett Miller Center of Public Affairs

The Honorable Herbert Brownell, Co-chairman
The Honorable Birch E. Bayh, Jr., Co-chairman

The Honorable Mortimer M. Caplin, Vice Chairman

The Honorable Philip W. Buchen
Chief Justice Warren E. Burger
The Honorable M. Caldwell Butler
Ms. Carolyne K. Davis
Ms. Nancy M. Neuman
Mrs. Karen O'Neil
Mr. Chalmers M. Roberts
Dr. M. Roy Schwarz
Mr. W. Reece Smith, Jr.
The Honorable William B. Spong, Jr.

Presidential Vacancy, Disability, and Inability

Twenty-fifth Amendment

SECTION 1. In case of the removal of the President from office or of his death or resignation, the Vice President shall become President.

SECTION 2. Whenever there is a vacancy in the office of the Vice President, the President shall nominate a Vice President who shall take office upon confirmation by a majority vote of both Houses of Congress.

SECTION 3. Whenever the President transmits to the President pro tempore of the Senate and the Speaker of the House of Representatives his written declaration that he is unable to discharge the powers and duties of his office, and until he transmits to them a written declaration to the contrary, such powers and duties shall be discharged by the Vice President as Acting President.

SECTION 4. Whenever the Vice President and a majority of either the principal officers of the executive departments or of such other body as Congress may by law provide, transmit to the President pro tempore of the Senate and the Speaker of the House of Representatives their written declaration that the President is unable to discharge the powers and duties of his office, the Vice President shall immediately assume the powers and duties of the office as Acting President.

Thereafter, when the President transmits to the President pro tempore of the Senate and the Speaker of the House of Representatives his written declaration that no inability exists, he shall resume the powers and duties of his office unless the Vice President and a majority of either the principle officers of the executive department or of such other body as Congress may by law provide, transmit within four days to the President pro tempore of the Senate and the Speaker of the House of Representatives their written declaration that the President is unable to discharge the powers and duties of his office. Thereupon Congress shall decide the issue, assembling within forty-eight hours for that purpose if not in session. If the Congress within twenty-one days after receipt of the latter written declaration, or, if Congress is not in session within twenty-one days after Congress is required to assemble, determines by two-thirds vote of both Houses that the President is unable to discharge the powers and duties of his office, the Vice President shall continue to discharge the same as Acting President; otherwise, the President shall resume the powers and duties of his office.

Note: Ratification completed February 10, 1967.

INTRODUCTION

Not until the ratification of the 25th Amendment to the Constitution on February 10, 1967, was the president, when he believed he was unable to discharge the duties of his office, authorized to make a temporary transfer of his powers and duties to the vice president. Set forth for the first time is the machinery for the vice president and a majority of the Cabinet, on their own initiative, to make this determination, with the vice president immediately thereafter assuming these powers and duties as acting president. If the president, however, challenges this unilateral action, he will prevail unless two-thirds of both houses of Congress confirm his inability so to perform. This Commission believes that, under most circumstances, the 25th Amendment is clear, simple and easily implemented. Certain of the Amendment's provisions, however, are designed to respond to extremely complicated circumstances and could prove to be more difficult to implement. Hence the Commission strongly urges steps to provide a guide for future applications of the 25th whether they be of a crisis nature or of a lesser nature, a guide that will assure prompt application in a manner faithful both to the spirit of the Constitution and to the intent of the framers of this amendment.

Above all, the Commission believes this is a time to "seize the moment." In 1988 Americans will choose a new president with the inauguration barely ten weeks later. During that critical, often frenetic, transition period many problems of policy and personnel must be resolved. Along with them, the potential problems of presidential disability and the use of this amendment must be discussed and, as far as humanly possible, agreed upon through contingency planning by the new president, vice president, presidential physician, and White House chief of staff. In all of this, there surely will be a role for the president's spouse. Most emphatically, this must be done not after inauguration but before.

Why the urgency? One example should suffice. Consider the testimony of Dr. Daniel Ruge who was President Reagan's physician on March 31, 1981, less than three months after his inauguration when a would-be

159

assassin seriously wounded the chief executive. Dr. Ruge was in Reagan's entourage that rushed with him to the hospital. When the Commission asked about the possible use of the 25th Amendment, he responded:

It was discussed. There is a big difference between Dan Ruge on March 30, 1981, after a shooting when he'd only been on the job two months for one thing and what Dan Ruge would have been like four years later [at the time of Reagan's colon cancer operation] when he would have actually had time from April 1981 to July 1985 to think about it. I think very honestly in 1981 because of the speed of everything and the fact that we had a very sick president that the 25th Amendment would never have entered my mind even though I probably had it in my little black bag. I carried it with me. The 25th Amendment never occurred to me.

Q: You think it would have occurred to you if the shooting had happened four years later?

Dr. Ruge: Yes.

Later, Dr. Ruge was asked:

Could the President have signed a letter [making the vice president the acting president] after he got to the hospital and was in the operating room?

Dr. Ruge replied:

Yes, he could have signed anything up until the time he went under anesthesia.

Clearly, there must be much greater public recognition that presidents, like the rest of us, are subject to periodic illnesses and disabilities and that the 25th Amendment, among other things, offers excellent standard operating procedures for times of temporary presidential disability, a simple method to get through such contingencies without disruption of government or public alarm.

The Commission has been impressed by what it has learned of the advances, and complexities, of modern medicine, in part by our discussions with two former presidential physicians who cared for five presidents. It is now obvious that the presidential physician can, and must, play an increased role. We view it as a dual role: first, the traditional one of confidential doctor-patient relationship, and second and equally important in the uniquely presidential case, a role as a representative, in strictly non-political terms, of the interests of the nation which elected the president. (This is discussed in greater detail in Annex A.)

These dual roles, as well as other aspects that are part of the history and potential of the 25th Amendment, especially in the often shadowy area of judgments about disability, including potentially long-term and chronic disability, are discussed in this report, together with specific recommendations.

Eight of the 35 men who have occupied the White House have died in office, four of them victims of assassins. Several have had serious illnesses, some of which at the time were hidden from those who should have been told, as well as from the public. We must be better prepared to cope with the frailties of man in this nuclear age; the national interest demands it; the 25th Amendment can help. We hope this report contributes to knowledge for decision making.

The 25th Amendment now has been embedded in the Constitution for more than 20 years. The Commission does not recommend any further constitutional changes at this time but it does point to some legislation it feels the Congress and the president should consider in order to bring current law into better harmony with the 25th Amendment and its intentions. Some sections of the 25th (numbers 1 and 2) already have come into play with no resulting problem though a potential problem is commented upon on page 6. The other sections (numbers 3 and 4), on which the bulk of this report centers, are, as we said at the beginning, designed to apply to complicated factual situations and are dependent to a great extent upon the circumstances which exist at the time of implementation. Thus scenarios for endless mischief have been constructed and widely printed as both fact and fiction, horror stories of what the 25th might produce·

It should be noted that during the consideration of the 25th Amendment, Congress considered a number of possible horror story scenarios. It concluded that the final language of the Amendment contained the least possibilities of malfunctioning. And further, it concluded that each effort to shore up potential weaknesses only made matters worse.

161

Because the 25th Amendment deals with the possibility of unpredictable human frailties, it is not perfect. In fact, there are no perfect solutions under such circumstances.

However, it is the Commission's opinion that rather than amend the Constitution in an attempt to deal with such presidential disability scenarios, political reality requires that the people of this nation must make the most of what the 25th Amendment encompasses. Given that as a fact, the Commission offers analyses and suggestions, most especially for the incoming chief executive, his vice president, and those who will aid and assist, as well as for the Congress and the public.

Throughout, the Commission has assumed that stability in time of crisis, or in any departure from what has been the norm, depends on the good judgment and the good sense of both our leaders and our citizens, regardless of their political associations. As the late Senate Republican leader Everett M. Dirksen put it during the deliberations about the 25th Amendment: "We must assume that, when confronted with monumental national crisis, when subjected to the white heat of political scrutiny, those charged with responsibility will do what is in the public interest."

The subject matter of this Commission overlaps at important points that of the Miller Center Commission on Presidential Transitions and Foreign Policy co-chaired by former Secretaries of State William P. Rogers and Cyrus R. Vance. The present Commission commends the close reading of the two reports as they interrelate with one another.

THE 25TH AMENDMENT

Section 1

Section 1 simply provides that in case of "the removal of the President from office or of his death or resignation, the Vice President shall become President." The basic language of this section is derived from Article II, Section 1, Clause 5 of the Constitution. Suffice it to say of Section 1 that "death" and "resignation" are such finite acts that Section 1 has presented no problems historically, since the first vice president to succeed a president, John Tyler after the death of William Henry Harrison, simply took the prescribed oath and proclaimed himself to be president, not acting president. This firm precedent has since been followed in seven cases and ended the early constitutional

162

question of whether the new occupant should be acting president or president.

Section 2

Section 2, like Section 1, relates to Article II, Section 1, Clause 5 of the Constitution but fills a major void, that is, what should be done when there is no sitting vice president as has been the case for some 20 per cent of our national history. Section 2 provides for presidential nomination, with congressional confirmation, of a vice president in case of a vacancy. This procedure now has been used twice: President Nixon on October 12, 1973, nominated Representative Gerald Ford following the resignation of Spiro T. Agnew and, only 10 months later, after Ford became president on Nixon's resignation, Ford on August 20, 1974, nominated former New York Governor Nelson A. Rockefeller to be vice president.

These vice presidential cases—and they were not unanticipated—gave the United States its first unelected president. But they were not quite as immediate and clear-cut exercises in the constitutional transfer of power as has been the case under Section 1. This is because Section 2 provides no time limits for presidential nomination or congressional debate and approval, by majority vote of both House and Senate, of a vice president. In the first case, Ford's nomination as vice president, was followed by confirmation 54 days after Nixon nominated him; in the second case, President Ford's nomination of Rockefeller, confirmation was not finally approved until 121 days after his nomination. The intervals between the occurrence of the vacancy and the presidential nomination to fill it also differed: In Ford's case, 3 days; in Rockefeller's case, 11 days.

There were, of course, good and, at the time, sufficient political if not public policy reasons for all these time periods. Still, one can conjure up possibilities of a presidential and vice presidential vacancy that the 25th Amendment does not address. For example, both the president and vice president could die in a common tragedy. In this event the Presidential Succession Act of 1947 would come into play because both the presidency and vice presidency would be vacant (Annex B). Some of this act's provisions are now in conflict with the superseding 25th Amendment and should be altered by Congress.

163

Section 3

Section 3 was a great leap forward into the unknown, an effort to provide a method of continuity at the top of our government, that is, in the presidency. It has, in the Commission's view, been used in a single instance, at the time of Reagan's hospitalization for colon cancer surgery, despite the fact that in the July 13, 1985 letter Reagan then signed he specifically stated that while he was "mindful of the provisions of Section 3," he did "not believe that the drafters of this Amendment intended its application to situations such as the instant one." He went on to say: "Nevertheless, consistent with my long-standing arrangement with Vice President George Bush, and not intending to set a precedent binding anyone privileged to hold this Office in the future," he was passing to the vice president his "powers and duties . . . commencing with the administration of anesthesia to me in this instance." The president concluded by saying he would advise the Senate's president pro tempore and the Speaker of the House (to whom the letter was addressed, under the terms of Article 3) "when I determine that I am able to resume the discharge of the constitutional powers and duties of this Office."

Fred F. Fielding, then counsel to President Reagan, in his testimony to the Commission said, in part, the following:

"Let's go back to the week before the operation. We knew—some of us knew—and I forget when it became public, that the President was going to have his physical. We knew at the time that he was going to have a form of anaesthesia, to have the procedure that occurred on Friday, if I recall my dates correctly. He was operated on Saturday, got a procedure on Friday. What was going to happen was that there was a possibility that if something was found that they would have to instantly put the President under. I used that as an opportunity the preceding week to schedule a meeting with the President and the vice president and Don Regan (then chief of staff). We sat in the Oval Office and we discussed the whole situation: the National Command Authority plus the President's desires on passage of power temporarily if he were suddenly temporarily incapacitated. . . .

"The decision was obvious that unless something unexpected occurred on Friday there would be no need for the 25th Amendment in any way, shape or

164

form. But Don Regan called me down late afternoon on that Friday and said "We've got some problems with the health exam." And we went through the whole drill—if you will—of what is to be done and where is the vice president, and what is the press to be advised of and what is not to be told, and the normal procedures that you go through. One of the subjects obviously was the 25th Amendment. I can tell you, and I think it is important for the sake of history, that when we left, no decision of a recommendation to the President had been made although we knew the procedures. I drafted basically two letters: one was a little flushing out of the letter that was already in the book,[*] and the other was basically the letter the President actually signed.

---

[*]At another point Fielding said to the Commission:

One of the things that I had my staff working on was a book, basically an emergency book. What do you do about X, Y, Z, events concerning the President's health? I state in all candor that [the book] was not completed on March 30. Early afternoon, and suddenly the President was shot and we all realized (a) it was an incident, (b) the President was shot, (c) it was very serious. The stories were many; we ultimately ended up in the basement room.

Everybody now is aware of the 25th Amendment. To be very frank with you, that day, when I mentioned the 25th Amendment I could see eyes glazing over in some parts of the Cabinet. They didn't even know about the 25th Amendment. It wasn't a full Cabinet meeting, it was whomever in the Cabinet could be notified, started drifting in and taking seats around the table.

The book is now finished. Whenever I would travel with the President there are two copies. I would always carry a copy with me of the book. There was always one back in my office in the safe. The book basically is every situation you can imagine that has occurred to the president or the vice president: it is, for that matter, scenarios.

I did that because I knew that there was reluctance on the part of the President to activate the 25th Amendment for a "minor" procedure of short-term duration . . . .

"I thought the President should have two options: one was very clear, that of exercise of the 25th Amendment; and the other was a piece that would accomplish the activation of the 25th Amendment, but was more consistent with what I perceived to be the President's concerns. His concern mainly was that he didn't want to set a precedent for future Presidents. But I can tell you in all candor there was no political reason why he didn't want to, which theoretically there could be as with someone who is having a power fight or whatever you would with their vice president.

"Next morning I sat down with the Chief of Staff at the hospital and we discussed this. I showed him the two drafts, the normal draft and the optional draft, and I don't think Don's mind was made up at that point, until that point, to be very honest. I think his mind was still open about it. We discussed it and then we went in and discussed it with the President in the hospital room. And he made his decision, he signed the optional paper. As it turned out, the doctor had predicted three hours for the operation. He wanted to get a little head start so he started the anaesthesia earlier than he had told us he was going to start it because he wanted to give himself a little more time. So there probably was a period of time in there, although it was academic, a technical period of time when the President was out, and we had not called Vice President Bush.

"Later that afternoon we asked to see the doctor. [The operating surgeon, not the presidential physician.] We explained to him the 25th Amendment, the implications of it. We explored it with him. I was asking questions about how you could know, what was the legitimate way to determine whether the President was capable, understanding, lucid, and that sort of thing. We hit upon several tests, one of which was that I said "I'm going to ask him to sign a letter. How about asking him to read the letter and understand it? Wouldn't that be evidence that he was lucid?" And he said, "Yep." We went in a little after seven to see him. He was joking with the nurses when we walked in. We had a conversation with him; we discussed the transfer of power. I handed him the letter and he picked it up and literally started to read it and his eyes were shutting and opening, and it was obviously going like this, like he was turning his eyes. And I thought, uh oh, and Don Regan and I looked at each other and decided that maybe we were a little premature. Then the President reminded us that he didn't have his glasses and he didn't have his contacts on and he couldn't read it. It had nothing to do with his consciousness at all. We read the letter to him; we discussed it with him. Don said something, in effect, "Now that you know what we are up to, Mr. President, maybe we'll come back in a couple of hours and ask you to sign it," when at that point the President said, (this is not a full quote, but something to the effect) "Oh, heck no, I don't want you to wake me up later. I'll sign it now." So we decided he was lucid enough, certainly, to take it back.

"My mind was that it should not be shorter than necessary or longer than required since this was the first exercise of the Amendment. I would have had no problem with going overnight with everything we knew and all the briefings that we had and all the strategic information we had. But in my mind, again, my own personal view was if you were comfortable with the President's condition, the sooner the better for any number of reasons. And certainly it was a very practical, political reason that the public out there needed reassurance the President was in fact really O.K., this wasn't a death-threatening situation, that he . . . had come through the procedure and was lucid enough to take back the problems.

"The worst thing in the world would have been to have him transfer—and this was the other thing we talked about—the power to the vice president, take it back, and then later have to transfer it back again. So that was a factor in our thinking as well. We had to be reassured by the doctors that the probabilities of that to occur was low.

167

"Our question was not was the man in discomfort. The question was whether he was lucid or whether he had the ability to carry on, not whether it was comfortable in the short term. When somebody asked whether the White House physician was in on the discussion, the answer was no. But I know that Don Regan talked to the doctor at that time and we had discussed the scenario with him the night before. It wasn't that the White House physician was excluded; it was that once we got into the surgery phase that we were dealing with the surgical team."[1]

The Commission believes that Section 3 of the 25th Amendment should have been used by Reagan and other presidents where anaesthesia is involved. The Commission believes that the best course is to make routine the use of this mechanism so that its invocation carries no implications of instability or crisis. Each president will have to make each decision and instances will be different. However, the Commission believes that use rather than non-use will create the sense of routine.

Section 3 creates a simple and relatively straightforward way for the president to provide for situations in which he suffers from a temporary inability to carry out the duties of office. The key aspects of this procedure are a determination by the president that he will be temporarily unable to perform, a communication of this determination to the speaker of the house and the president pro tempore of the Senate, and a subsequent communication from the president that his inability has ended. In cases where the president knows in advance he will enter into a period of inability, this mechanism permits a smooth transition of power under the president's ultimate control.

It should be possible to identify in advance a fairly wide range set of circumstances where the president should almost automatically invoke Section 3. One situation involves elective surgery where a general anesthetic, narcotics, or other drugs that alter cerebral function will be used. Another involves a similarly debilitating disease or physical malfunction. Because anyone under anesthetic is unable to function both during the period of unconsciousness and afterwards while disoriented, presidents should accept the inevitability of a temporary transfer of power to the vice president that would extend beyond the immediate hours in the operating room, or even in the hospital, perhaps 24 or 48 hours. It would be wise for a president to state this publicly so that the nation and the world is reassured and, importantly so that the pressure is lessened on those White House officials fearful of some loss of power.

In short, let the president wave from his window to show he is up and around but convalescing while the vice president, as acting president under Section 3, takes care of the day-to-day business. As Herbert Brownell has noted there is a substantial difference between the president being able to wave to the crowd from a hospital window and being able to govern.

The president is the only person with the power and prerogative to invoke or not invoke Section 3. Thus far the question of using Section 3 has been raised two times due to presidential illness. The Commission was told that the "non use" of Section 3 was determined by the White House staff after the attempted assassination of Reagan and by Reagan and the White House staff prior to his cancer surgery. The White House physician was not consulted by the White House staff before the emergency surgery following the attempted assassination, although he was inside the hospital. Prior to the cancer surgery, the White House staff received inadequate medical information or chose to ignore the information it did receive.

The Commission reemphasizes that during the transition period between election and inauguration the new president, vice president, presidential physician and chief of staff should consider what to do in contingencies of a medical nature. The Commission recommends written guidelines if possible, agreed upon in advance,[2] under which Section 3 could or would be invoked for three levels of medical conditions—an emergency, a planned procedure, or treatment for a chronic ailment. Most certainly, it should be invoked for any surgical procedure involving the use of anesthesia, narcotics and other drugs which alter cerebral function. In judging the president's ability to resume the powers and duties of office, consideration must be given to anything that impairs mental capacities.

The advice of the presidential physician is especially important because the president may otherwise not appreciate the extent to which particular medical situations may compromise his ability to function. As part of the

169

periodic review of the president's health, he and his physician should consider whether any new situations should be added to the list of contingencies that may involve disability.

In cases of elective surgery and similar circumstances, the president will have no difficulty invoking Section 3. There may arise situations, however, where an unanticipated medical crisis places the president in a position where he, his vice president, chief of staff and physician had previously agreed to rely on Section 3. President Reagan's surgery following the assassination attempt is just such a case. The president-elect, his vice president, chief of staff and physician should, at the earliest possible date, try to design special rules to cover such a crisis if and when it occurs.

One possibility would be for the president-elect to prepare an appropriate letter for invoking Section 3, which he could leave unsigned and undated. Under agreed-upon conditions, such as an imminent general anesthetic or an injury resulting in impending shock or loss of consciousness, Secret Service personnel or others accompanying the president (as could well have been the case with Dr. Ruge, already discussed) could produce the letter for his signature. This plan of action could be used, of course, only in cases where the president remained conscious and competent at the time he signed the letter. Although this prospect of shifting presidential power under emergency conditions might strike some as unsettling, the Commission believes that such a formula is preferable to putting the vice president and the Cabinet to the choice of invoking Section 4 or leaving the office of the president effectively unoccupied.

The Commission recognizes that a president facing a "grey area" medical situation—a case where his inability is likely to be transitory—may prefer to do nothing on the assumption that any transfer of power can erode the appearance of his authority even where it does not affect its actual exercise. In many cases, however, a wait-and-see attitude carries unacceptable risks. Even the most straightforward medical procedure, if conducted under general anesthesia, can lead to complications. The patient can suddenly stop breathing or undergo cardiac arrest, either in response to the surgery or to the anesthesia. The patient may simply remain unconscious much longer than anticipated, or remain confused after regaining

170

consciousness. The Commission is concerned that instances have occurred where officials in an administration have overestimated the president's ability to perform his duties without the proper interval following anesthesia.

Rather than run the risk of leaving a power vacuum, the Commission recommends that in borderline cases the president take the precaution of using Section 3 by designating the vice president as acting president. Once the public comes to accept this course as a normal way of doing business, the perception problem will disappear. By showing strong leadership here a president could increase his stature in history as well as aid his successors in office. We believe that the president can count on the good sense and good judgment of the American people, the Congress and his immediate colleagues in such situations.

The Commission has heard four reasons for not invoking Section 3. The first is that a president who invokes its provisions would set a precedent for future presidents. (This was the case in Reagan's letter of July 13, 1985.) The second is that to invoke it would contribute to a crisis atmosphere that might alarm friends and allies abroad, mislead our adversaries and cause serious reactions in the financial community, even a stock market crash. The third is that the casual use of Section 3 might tempt the vice president or others to undertake a coup by employing Section 4 to seize presidential powers. The fourth reason is the skepticism in political circles over whether medical information is or can be precise enough to determine with any degree of certainty the disability of the president.

The Commission examined, in turn, these four viewpoints and rejected each of them. First of all, Section 3 leaves to each president the determination of whether or not to invoke it. Its use is strictly voluntary. Second, the risk of a crisis atmosphere is proportionate to the degree to which a natural and orderly routine for the transfer of powers is institutionalized, that is, widely understood and generally accepted by the public. Thus the more the provision is used by succeeding presidents, the more routine it becomes and the less sense of crisis there will be at home and abroad. Third, the fear of a coup by a vice president is based on a false analogy with other political systems. Historically the defects of the American vice presidency have not been the temptation to seize power but the refusal to accept power inherent in the office.

Examples are Vice President Chester Arthur during the long illness of President James Garfield after an assassin shot him and Vice President Thomas Marshall during President Woodrow Wilson's grave illness. After President Eisenhower's 1955 heart attack, Vice President Nixon scrupulously avoided any act not clearly authorized by the President. In Nixon's case, and ever since, the tempo of modern communications has assured wide and swift public disclosure of the least sign of a "power grab." Fourth and finally, this same modern communications technology, and the media habits that have grown with it, make it far less likely that physicians to presidents could successfully hide illnesses as was true in varying degrees during the presidencies of Grover Cleveland, Woodrow Wilson, Franklin D. Roosevelt and John F. Kennedy. Eisenhower and Reagan, two presidents who suffered a number of well known illnesses while in office, either voluntarily or by media pressure, or both, responded with disclosure. This is not to say that public suspicion of medical cover-ups has disappeared, or ever will, but it surely lessens that possibility. And as public understanding has grown of the uses and reach of modern medicine, including anesthesia as the Commission has been repeatedly told, a cover-up carries political as well as physical risks to those who would opt for it.

One issue the Commission considered is the advisability of written agreements between a president and his vice president by which the president would in effect delegate his Section 3 authority under certain specified circumstances. Through such an agreement the president would declare his intent that if a particular situation arose as a result of which he lost his capacity to determine his ability to function, the vice president would have the authority to inform the speaker of the house and the president pro tempore of the Senate that an inability existed and that he would serve as acting president until the president recovered. Before the adoption of the 25th Amendment, similar agreements existed between Presidents Eisenhower, Kennedy and Johnson and their respective vice presidents, although no occasion arose to test their efficacy or validity.

Whatever the constitutional status of those agreements that antedated the 25th Amendment, the Commission believes that such delegations no longer are appropriate. The

Commission regards the constitutionality of such agreements as an open question in the sense that there is no definitive authority on point. However, it seems likely that such an agreement would be inconsistent with the 25th Amendment. One could assert that the express authority of Section 3 carries with it implicit power to anticipate in advance when that power will be exercised. More persuasive to the Commission is the argument that Section 4 provides the exclusive means for determining a presidential inability once the president loses the capacity to make that determination for himself. When the Constitution so clearly and directly addresses an issue—here the mechanism for temporary transfers of power from the president to the vice president—efforts to find alternative, implicit resolutions seem forced.

Because the principal purpose of the 25th Amendment is to resolve all doubts over the status of the chief executive during periods of crisis or uncertainty, the Commission considers it unwise and contrary to the Amendment's spirit to rely on a method not clearly contemplated by the Amendment. In coming to this conclusion, the Commission of course offers no judgment on the binding effect of such agreements during the period before adoption of the 25th Amendment. The history of the Amendment indicates that its framers intended to create a mechanism that would supersede those prior strategies, and that they did not intend either to repudiate or merely to supplement the earlier arrangements.

In short, Section 3 creates a constitutional mechanism within the 25th Amendment for a president to say, in effect, that "I am unable to serve temporarily. Rather than resign the office, I will temporarily remove myself and have the vice president serve as acting president. When I am able again to serve I will reclaim the presidency." This is the pattern Reagan followed in July 1985 during his surgery, despite the disclaimer in his letter. The testimony to this Commission of his then counsel, Fred Fielding, shows invocation of Section 3 was his and his associates' clear intent; the disclaimer simply was a device, offered the president as an alternative, to get him at least to start
down the Section 3 route. And that is how it worked out.

173

Section 4

Section 4 is the most tantalizing and so far the only unused provision of the 25th Amendment. It deals with a crisis which our nation has never directly confronted although, in retrospect, it probably could have applied to the final period of Woodrow Wilson's presidency or of Franklin D. Roosevelt's.

In brief, this provision involves a sick president who refuses or is unable to confront his disability. Put another way, this section was basically framed to apply to a president who is disabled but unwilling to step aside. He or she may be a "stubborn mule," or be in the hands of a powerful staff or of a strong willed spouse, the latter as in Wilson's case. In that case, the presidential physician was Mrs. Wilson's witting accomplice.

Prior to the 25th Amendment, other than impeachment, there was no mechanism for dealing with an unfit president who would not resign, or who was not mentally capable of resigning his office. Impeachment, however, was designed to deal with high crimes and misdemeanors, not health problems. In contrast, Section 4 has inspired much criticism and many scenarios for endless mischief. The effect of modern medicine on human life certainly has increased the imaginable scenarios. For reasons such as these Congress deliberated at great length before approving Section 4 in order to erect what might be called a large enough constitutional tent, with plenty of room inside to accommodate all possible cases, whether foreseen, completely unforeseen or simply imagined.

It is essential, too, in assessing this section's potential use, to remember that no mechanical or procedural solution would be failsafe unless the public possesses, at such a time of crisis, a certain sense of "constitutional morality." Or, as another observer has put it: "In a word, the Amendment is only technically self-executing. Nonetheless, it contains all that a constitutional device should: a set of presumptions about the process of exercising power and an implicit expectation that it will be applied in a mood of restraint."[3]

Section 4 operates in two stages. First of all, there has to be the momentous decision to remove the president and make the vice president the acting president. This decision requires the declaration of the vice president and of a majority of the president's Cabinet. A situation might

174

also arise if the president having temporarily transferred his powers to the vice president sought to resume his powers by transferring written declarations to the Senate and House but was then prevented by the vice president and the Cabinet declaring him unable to discharge his duties.

Beyond this, Section 4 also has built into it the authority for Congress to create some other "body" to substitute for the Cabinet. There is no limitation on who would serve in such a "body" other than the realities of American politics and public opinion and that sense of "constitutional morality," which is most essential at a time of national crisis. However, if such other "body" were set up, a majority of the members of that body would need to take the initiative or concur with the vice president in order to transfer temporarily the powers and duties of the presidency to the vice president. The Cabinet would play no role in this process, if Congress were to enact a statute creating such a body. Thus, it lies within the power of Congress to consider whether the Cabinet is the best decision-making group to be involved in a determination of presidential inability.

Various groups, other than the Cabinet, were suggested during the hearings leading up to the formulation of the 25th Amendment, and they continue to be suggested. Suggestions for the "other body" include, for example, a group composed of the chief justice, the speaker of the house, the president pro tempore of the Senate, and the minority leaders of both houses of Congress. Another suggestion is that this "other body" be composed of medical doctors either appointed for terms of years or designated by office, such as the surgeon general. The concern underlying all of these suggestions for some body other than the Cabinet is that, while the Cabinet members are apt to be loyal to the administration and have first hand awareness of the president's condition, they are also likely to be overly reluctant to acknowledge publicly that the president has any deficiencies. In other words, the Cabinet's lack of detached objectivity and its unwillingness to act on this question are plausible. Therefore, the argument goes, the public interest requires that the question of the president's ability to perform the duties of his office be evaluated by a group able to view the question in a more disinterested way.

The Commission has considered whether to propose that Congress exercise its power under Section 4 to create a body other than the Cabinet for this purpose. In this process, the Commission has reviewed the various arguments and proposals made in the hearings leading up to the framing of the Amendment, as well as current proposals, and has concluded not to recommend the creation of some other statutory body. The Commission recognizes that although the Cabinet does suffer from the defects mentioned above, and may not be an ideal group, it is unlikely that any other body could be designed that would be free of other difficulties or receive as much political acceptance. It would seem desirable that, whatever group is employed, consultation could usefully take place with the White House physician, with the help and assistance of outside medical specialists.

Even if Congress does not create a permanent body of this sort, this provision in Section 4 is salutary in that it gives Congress power to act if, in a particular situation, the Cabinet fails to act where it is clear that the president is suffering from an inability. At that point, Congress could create another body to take action in that special situation. Such congressional action would be subject to presidential veto as any other legislation and a veto could be overridden by a two-thirds vote of both houses. Such a body would be temporary and tailor-made for a one-time only assignment, leaving the Cabinet in place as the body to deal with other situations thereafter.

The Commission strongly believes that the chief justice and other members of the Supreme Court should have no role in any such "body" or in any other fashion under terms of the 25th Amendment. The late Chief Justice Earl Warren advised strongly against any such role during deliberations in Congress on the amendment and former Chief Justice Warren Burger took the same position in speaking to the Commission. The Commission considers it essential to keep separate the judicial role lest, in a situation perhaps now unimaginable, the Supreme Court might be called on to rule on some application of the 25th Amendment. Historically, it is worth recalling the presidential election crisis of 1876, in which only two days before inauguration day Rutherford B. Hayes prevailed over Samuel J. Tilden and then only by a vote of a congressionally-appointed electoral commission of seven Republican, seven Democrats, and one "independent"—five of whom were senators, five representatives and five justices of the Supreme Court.

Four of the justices were selected by the Congress and the fifth, the "independent", by the four. This fifth justice, Joseph P. Bradley, cast the deciding vote in the 8-to-7 ruling. It is true that concurrent political bargaining over the underlying post-Civil War issues provided the essential resolution of the crisis but the Court was misused in the role it did play.

The essential person in any application of the 25th Amendment's Section 4 is the vice president, the Cabinet or "other body" notwithstanding. The vice president cannot be substituted. Nor can the vice president become the acting president if the president objects unless the vice president affirmatively joined in the declaration initiating that procedure. In the latter case, the president can then object. In situations where the president is simply unconscious or incommunicado obviously no objection is possible. If the president is seriously ill and does not realize it, as was arguably Wilson's situation and, it is now widely recognized, was Franklin D. Roosevelt's in the final period of his 12 years in the White House, it is possible the president would object.

If the president, despite the vice president's joint action taken with a majority of the Cabinet or "other body," declares that "no inability" exists and is therefore reclaiming the presidency, Congress becomes the referee. It would take a two-thirds vote of both Senate and House to uphold the vice presidential claim in the face of an objecting president.

Any Section 4 action would place a vice president on the hottest of political hot seats, especially if there were to be any public doubt about the president's condition. The history of the vice presidency with its limited constitutionally prescribed role has not been a happy one; "a spare tire on the automobile of government," was one of the more polite descriptions by John Nance Garner who occupied the post eight years. Now the 25th Amendment's Section 4 places the major and most positive burden on the vice president in any removal of the president from office. A vice president is likely to be apprehensive about the appearance of disloyalty or of self-aggrandizement. Thus despite knowledge of the true condition of the president, the vice president, in such a case, most likely would feel ambivalent. The Commission believes that it makes good political and common sense to relieve him, or her, of as much of the resulting ambivalence as possible in having to be the initiator of the very process leading to his or her own self-promotion to the highest office in the land. Although it is clear that Section 4 provides an equal role for the vice president and the Cabinet, it is also true that to the extent the Cabinet is willing to play an active and visible role in the Section 4 process, the vice president is placed in a less difficult position.

Given current medical knowledge of the disabilities of older persons, the current prominence at all ages of psychiatric as well as physical illnesses and the progressive impairment of mental functions including the so-far irreversible disease known as Alzheimer's, the scenarios to which Section 4 might in the future apply can only be imagined. The Commission discussed such problem areas with both the former presidential physicians and other medical authorities available to it. Knowledge has only reinforced the Commission's feeling that the future cannot be better provided for by any new law, or even constitutional amendment, it might now suggest. But some established regime might help, especially those involving the presidential physician.

It is obvious that the presidential physician would be a critical person should Section 4 ever have to be considered. A vice president and Cabinet, or "other body," would be highly dependent on medical advice in reaching what would be, nonetheless, basically a political decision. (An annex to this paper goes into detail as to the Commission's view of the role of the presidential physician and what can, and should, be done now to enhance his standing.)

There are other persons to be considered, notably the president's spouse and the president's White House chief of staff and entourage.

Thus far presidential spouses have all been wives. Many have been apolitical, several politically influential, some powerful in terms, as they have seen it, of protecting their husband's health and political fortunes. Sometimes this has led to hiding presidential illnesses, the most obvious 20th century case being that of Edith Bolling Wilson during her husband's final years of semi-invalidism in the White House after suffering successive strokes. In that case the presidential physician colluded with Mrs. Wilson to hide the truth from almost everyone.

178

Of course, voters do not elect presidential spouses but historically first ladies have had their own individually differing roles and, in recent years, their own staff and offices. The Commission cannot and does not suggest any set of rules or code of conduct for future presidential spouses but it does strongly recommend that each be brought into the preparatory transition discussions, already noted, on the possible applications of the 25th Amendment. It is essential that each, like the other key personnel around the president, be mentally prepared for what could occur, and unfortunately so often has occurred, and that each be familiar with the Amendment's provisions. The vice president's spouse also should be knowledgeable about the 25th and its potential applications.

The presidential chief of staff, a post whose concept was brought into the White House by President Eisenhower from his years of commanding allied forces in Europe during World War II, has become a critical cog in the executive branch. In recent years it has proved more important than any of even the more senior of the Cabinet departments, including State and Defense.

When Reagan was struck by a would-be assassin's bullet and rushed into surgery, the Commission has been told it was White House staff members who made the decision not to put before him the option of involving Section 3. In the case of the President's colon cancer surgery it was the President's decision not to officially invoke Section 3 but to use its form nonetheless—but the options offered him were those of key White House staff members.

The White House staff understandably sees an important role for itself in assessing presidential disability. Key members of the staff and in particular the chief of staff and immediate associates are in continuous contact with the president. They consider themselves uniquely qualified in judging the president's capacity for exercising powers and duties. They are conscious of their prerogatives, fearful of threats to the president's authority and cognizant of the high stakes of political power. The White House staff has the most to lose if and when the president relinquishes his powers. Particularly in some presidencies, the staff carries major responsibility for the details of administering and managing the presidency. Top staffers are likely to worry that the vice president, in the role of acting president, is less likely than they to know and do what the president would have wanted if not disabled. Worst fate of all, in the view of the White House staff, would be for the acting president to bring in assistants from the vice presidential staff.

When a president cannot perform the duties of the office, the nation and the government, if it lacks an acting president, may incur no serious difficulty for some time, especially if the president's incapacity escapes public attention. The staff can always appear to act for the president except to sign or veto bills passed by Congress, to submit nominations for Senate consideration or fill interim vacancies, to grant pardons, to make treaties, or to serve as commander in chief of the armed forces. However, a president in office should not encourage staff assistants ever to believe they can function without a president in place who with full consciousness bears responsibility for their actions. Otherwise, when the truth about a president's hidden incapacity becomes generally known, as inevitably happens, the decisions and policies which had been attributed to the ailing president become suspect and the standing of the presidency for that period in history becomes shaken. Also, just as happens whenever an administration practices deceit of any kind on the public, the office of the president loses stature and respect.

Wherever he goes, a president is accompanied by sure signs of the unremitting responsibilities which the office puts upon its holder. In these times, a president is never away from means of instant communications with any department of the United States government and with the head of almost any foreign government, and always within reach is the "football" containing secret codes that enable the president to signal an immediate response by this country if ever it should face a nuclear attack. Even while asleep, a president is subject to call at any time, and his aides will be rightfully criticized if, upon learning of a major calamity or an alarming threat to the nation, they do not inform the president immediately.

Such well-known aspects of the office and the worldwide prestige which the American presidency earns in advance for each new incumbent have given rise to extraordinary public expectations of what any person with the immense power of that office can and would do to cope with a sudden national emergency or world crisis. To keep and preserve the respect which the American public and people everywhere have for the capacity and dependability of the American presidency is an important reason for not deliberately permitting an official hiatus, however brief. If the president becomes unconscious or otherwise disabled and the vice president were not duly authorized to act, the circumstance that no person with the authority and power of a president is present and capable of acting does in itself debase the importance and value of the presidency. Much more harmful, to be sure, would be the effect if a national emergency or world crisis were actually to erupt during a hiatus. Such considerations, among others, ought to convince every responsible aide to a president that whenever or however a situation arises for applying the 25th Amendment, he or she must not dissemble about the president's health or otherwise fend off use of the constitutional remedy for a presidential illness. In addition, the American people must understand that their presidents, whoever they may be, are not supermen. They are human beings subjected to enormous pressures and responsibilities who, like the average citizen, may be confronted with disabling infirmities. However, the Commission believes that the 25th Amendment provides the means of insuring that the powers and duties of the presidency are always in the hands of one able to perform them. And the Commission believes that this Amendment must be utilized whenever necessary as a normal ingredient in the governmental process.

ENDNOTES

[1]From Fred F. Fielding's testimony to the Commission on September 30, 1986.

[2]Logically, this would be an expanded version of the "emergency book" created by Fred Fielding in the early Reagan years. (See footnote on page 8 of this report.)

[3]Richard P. Longaker, "Presidential Continuity: the Twenty-fifth Amendment," *13 UCLA Law Review 1966*, p. 560, cited in the forthcoming *Hidden Illness in the White House* by Kenneth R. Crispell, M.D. and Carlos F. Gomez, B.Sc. with C. Brian Kelly, p. 313.

ANNEX A

THE PRESIDENT'S PHYSICIAN

In the *1981 Congressional Directory*, the first issued during the Reagan administration, the staff listing for the Executive Office of the President (that is, the White House office) contained 55 names. They began with the counselor to the president, the chief of staff, his deputy, a raft of varied assistants to the president, then deputy assistants and special assistants. The last name on the list was the chief usher; the name just before his—54th of 55—was that of the physician to the president, preceded by the curator of White House artifacts.

This Commission has been shocked at the low rank and, sometimes, the seemingly low esteem accorded to the physician—and not just in the current administration.

Dr. Ruge, Reagan's first White House physician, told this Commission that "despite its glamorous name, the office of the White House physician is somewhat blue collar."

But it is far easier to say the physician's job should be upgraded than to suggest how to do it. This Commission has talked with Dr. William Lukash who served Presidents Johnson, Nixon, Ford and Carter as well as with other eminent and knowledgeable figures in both medicine and the structure and workings of the White House office. It is apparent that each president has his own habits in relation with his physician and that these have varied almost as greatly as have presidential foreign and domestic policies.

This leads us to conclude, first of all, that the president's physician must remain a person of the president's own choice, that he or she should not be subject to confirmation by the Senate or to approval by any other body, medical or otherwise. The president and his personal physician must have total mutual confidence and confidentiality, as a symbiotic relationship. But each of them must also realize that the physician has a dual obligation. As Dr. Lukash agreed, such physicians are "accepting a dual loyalty to their own patients but also to the public."

Further, it should be noted, the post of physician to the president has grown from a one-doctor role to what Dr. Lukash called providing "health care for the fifteen hundred constituents in the White House," with a second medical office in the adjoining Executive Office Building and "two assistant physicians to help with the traveling" groups which go with a chief executive, including the Secret Service, the press, the military and those involved in communications.

Still, the 25th Amendment centers directly on the president and, under certain circumstances, the vice president. This is the role being considered in this annex. All other medical functions are strictly secondary.

We must, and do, assume that any future physician to a president will not only be a skilled professional but be highly knowledgeable of both the medical and political aspects of the 25th Amendment. He or she must consider that he or she, and all those physicians who assist from time to time, are responsible not only for the care of the chief executive but also for the "care of the country."

To be an effective personal physician, the time honored concept of patient-doctor confidentiality must be in broad terms maintained. The physician must become acquainted with the vice president and have unquestioned access to the president.

The Commission suggests that a possible "code of conduct" for the president's physician should include:

a. From the beginning of his appointment, the physician must have a knowledge of the history, medical and political implications, and use of the 25th Amendment.

b. He or she should abide by the views of the American Medical Association Council on Medical Ethics regarding patient-doctor confidentiality and those instances when it can be abridged in the national or community interest. The Commission considered recommending a statute stating that the presidential physician had a positive duty to communicate details concerning the president's condition if it jeopardized the national interest but concluded that such a statute was not necessary and probably would be self-defeating.

c. He or she should meet during the transition period with the president-elect regarding the potential use of the disability provisions of the 25th Amendment. The physician should undertake during the transition with the president-elect, the vice president-elect, and those who will become the president's chief of staff and, legal counsel to establish, if possible, a written protocol regarding the use of these provisions.

d. He or she should possess the knowledge, humility and the expertise to obtain consultation to insure the best medical care for the president. Any presidential physician, if only because of his office, has easy access to any consultant or group of consultants that he wished to have see the president to aid in treatment or to make the difficult decision of evaluating disability, the latter being the key issue to invoke or not invoke Section 4.

In order to reinforce the influence of the president's physician whenever the 25th Amendment might come into play, it has been suggested by numerous persons and in various studies that an independent board of physicians be created to examine the president's physical and mental health from time to time. This concept was discussed by the commission and by the medical advisory group to the commission. The general conclusion was that while such a board would officially "protect" the President's physician, it would prevent or hinder a real doctor-patient relationship between the president and his or her physician.

The political and world situation, the power of the White House staff, and most of all the wishes of the President will always determine when and how Section 3 will be used. We urge that, because of his or her unique status, the president's physician, with consultants if he or she desires, play a major role. The physician should help the president make the decision to invoke Section 3 and to reassume office if the Amendment is used.

ANNEX B

Act of July 18, 1947

(a) (1) If, by reason of death, resignation, removal from office, inability, or failure to qualify, there is neither a president nor vice president to discharge the powers and duties of the office of president, then the speaker of the House of Representatives shall, upon his resignation as speaker and as representative in Congress, act as president.

(2) The same rule shall apply in the case of the death, resignation, removal from office, or inability of an individual acting as president under this subsection.

(b) If, at the time when under subsection (a) of this section a speaker is to begin the discharge of the powers and duties of the office of president, there is no speaker, or the speaker fails to qualify as acting president, then the president pro tempore of the Senate shall, upon his resignation as president pro tempore and as senator, act as president.

(c) An individual acting as president under subsection (a) or subsection (b) of this section shall continue to act until the expiration of the then current presidential term, except that—

(1) If his discharge of the powers and duties of the office is founded in whole or in part on the failure of both the president-elect and the vice president-elect to qualify, then he shall act only until a president or vice president qualifies; and

(2) If his discharge of the powers and duties of the office is founded in whole or in part on the inability of the president or vice-president, then he shall act only until the removal of the disability of one of such individuals.

(d) (1) If, by reason of death, resignation, removal from office, inability, or failure to qualify, there is no president pro tempore to act as president under subsection (b) of this section, then the officer of the United States who is highest on the following list, and who is not under disability to discharge the powers and duties of the office of president shall act as president: secretary of state, secretary of the treasury, secretary of defense, attorney general, postmaster general, secretary of the interior, secretary of agriculture, secretary of commerce, secretary of labor.[*]

(2) An individual acting as president under this subsection shall continue so to do until the expiration of the then current presidential term, but not after a qualified and prior-entitled individual is able to act, except that the removal of the disability of an individual higher on the list contained in paragraph (1) of this subsection or the ability to qualify on the part of an individual higher on such list shall not terminate his service.

(3) The taking of the oath of office by an individual specified in the list in paragraph (1) of this subsection shall be held to constitute his resignation from the office by virtue of the holding of which he qualifies to act as president.

(3) Subsections (a), (b), and (d) of this section shall apply only to such officers as are eligible to the office of president under the Constitution. Subsection (d) of this section shall apply only to officers appointed, by and with the advice and consent of the Senate, prior to the time of death, resignation, removal from office, inability, or failure to qualify, of the president pro tempore, and only to officers not under impeachment by the House of Representatives at the time the powers and duties of the office of president devolve upon them.

(F) During the period that any individual acts as president under this section, his compensation shall be at the rate then provided by law in the case of the president.

Act of January 19, 1886

Be it enacted by the Senate and House of Representatives of the United States of America in Congress assembled, That in case of removal, death, resignation, or

---

[*]The position of postmaster general was abolished in 1970, and the secretaries of health, education and welfare, of housing and urban development, and of transportation have been added to the line of succession.

inability of both the president and vice president of the United States, the secretary of state, or if there be none, or in case of his removal, death, resignation, or inability, then the secretary of the treasury, or if thee be none, or in case of his removal, death, resignation, or inability, then the secretary of War, or if there by none, or in case of his removal, death, resignation, or inability, then the attorney-general, or if there be none, or in the case of his removal, death, resignation, or inability then the postmaster general, or if there be none, or in case of his removal, death, resignation, or inability, then the secretary of the navy, of if there be none, or in case of his removal, death resignation, or inability, then the secretary of the interior, shall act as president until the disability of the president or vice president is removed or a president shall be elected: *Provided*, That whenever the powers and duties of the office of president of the United States shall devolve upon any of the persons named herein, if Congress be not then in session, or if it would not meet in accordance with law within twenty days thereafter, it shall be the duty of the person upon whom said powers and duties shall devolve to issue a proclamation convening Congress in extraordinary session, giving twenty days' notice of the time of meeting.

Sec. 2.   That the preceding section shall only be held to describe and apply to such officers as shall have been appointed by the advice and consent of the Senate to the offices therein named, and such as are eligible to the office of president under the Constitution, and not under impeachment by the House of Representatives of the United States at the time the powers and duties of the office shall devolve upon them respectively.

Sec. 3.   That sections one hundred and forty-six, one hundred and forty-seven, one hundred and forty-eight, one hundred and forty-nine, and one hundred and fifty of the Revised Statutes are hereby repealed.

Act of March 1, 1792

Sec. 9.   *And be it further enacted*, That in case of removal, death, resignation or inability both of the president and vice president of the United States, the president of the Senate pro tempore, and in case there shall be no president of the Senate [pro tempore], then the speaker of the House of Representatives, for the time being shall act as president of the United States until the disability be removed or a president shall be elected.

Sec. 10. *And be it further enacted*, That whenever the offices of president and vice president shall both become vacant, the secretary of state shall forthwith cause a notification thereof to be made to the executive of every state, and shall also cause the same to be published in at least one of the newspapers printed in each state, specifying that electors of the president of the United States shall be appointed or chosen in the several states within thirty-four days preceding the first Wednesday in December then next ensuing: *Provided*, There shall be the space of two months between the date of such notification and the said first Wednesday in December, but if there shall not be the space of two months between the date of such notification and the first Wednesday in December; and if the term for which the president and vice president last in office were elected shall not expire on the third day of March next ensuing, then the secretary of state shall specify in the notification that the electors shall be appointed or chosen within thirty-four days preceding the first Wednesday in December in the year next ensuing, within which time the electors shall accordingly be appointed or chosen, and the electors shall meet and give their votes on the first Wednesday in December, and the proceedings and duties of the said electors and others shall be pursuant to the directions prescribed in this act.